THINK for YOUR CUSTOMER

John and Linda Stanley

With Best wishes
John Stanley

lizardpublishing.biz

Published by lizardpublishing.biz, PO Box 604, Kalamunda,
Western Australia, 6926, Australia

National Library of Australia
Catalogue-in-Publication data:

Stanley, John Barry, 1948- .
Think for your customer.

ISBN 0 9750118 1 2.

1. Customer relations. 2. Customer services. I. Stanley,
Linda Sally, 1952- . II. Title.

658.812

Set in 10/12 Syntax
Design, layout and illustrations by 4L Design, Perth Western Australia

Printed in Singapore

Contents

SECTION 1

Introduction 1
    Train the Team to be Consistent 10
    It's Time to Change the Culture 14
    Walk the Customer's Journey 17
    Create an Experience 20

SECTION 2

Understanding the Selling Process 23
    Interruption Marketing versus Permission Marketing 25
    The Selling Formulae 26
    Emotional Marketing 29

SECTION 3

How to Become an Effective Host
  – Your Moment of Truth 35
      Body Language 36

SECTION 4

How to Become an Effective Consultant
  – Talk to Me and Build a Relationship 43
      Building a Relationship in One Sentence 47
      Become A Power Spot Promoter As Well! 49

SECTION 5

How to Become an Effective Salesperson
  – I Dare You to Close the Sale 55
      Become a Matchmaker 60
      Think and Drink 62
      Think FOR Your Customers 66

SECTION 6

Everyone Is Different 71
    Toddlers 72
    Teenagers 73
    Generation X 74
    Baby-Boomers 75
    Provide What the Customer Expects and You Will Fail 80
    Delight Your Customers 81

SECTION 7

Building Ongoing Relationships 87
   Do Consumers Trust Retailers? 88
   Send Birthday Cards, Don't Send Christmas Cards 92
   Newsletters — the '7 minute read' 94
   Say "Thank You" with a Thank You Card 96
   Yes, I Will Complain 100

SECTION 8

Praise the Team, Not the Customer 113

SECTION 9

Take Yourself Forward Five Years 119
   Welcome to Your New World! 120

About the Authors 124

Frequently Asked Questions 125
   Testimonials 127

SECTION 1

Introduction

Introduction

Customer service is constantly evolving. Why? Because the expectations we have when dealing with businesses are constantly changing — hence this book. *'Think FOR Your Customers'* is not simply another book on customer service. *Think FOR Your Customers* evolved out of my seminar presentations. It takes customer service several steps further, providing a more sophisticated framework for today's time-poor business person. This book considers the whole subject of customer service and is intended to stimulate your thoughts on the need for change in a rapidly changing world. This book will provide ideas for anyone who has customers and who feels the need to constantly develop his relationship with those customers.

We now live in a world that is more stressed by global events than it has been for over fifty years. Not only are we stressed by these global situations *per se*, but also how they affect our daily lives.

Leisure time is now at a premium as we work longer hours and try to compress more tasks into limited so-called 'free' time.

In addition to this, we have information overload. As a result, we are relying more heavily on experts to help us make decisions as the information needed to make a decision is becoming too complicated to enable us to make a sound judgement.

All of this means that business operations and customer care procedures need to change. As business operators the key is to *'Think FOR Your Customers'*, not to think *like* them.

Loyalty and trust are now the key ingredients of the customer-business relationship. Historically this has always been the case, although many companies lost sight of the importance of this with the emergence of self-service. However, in the new millennium, digital technology means we have the tools to rebuild this trust and loyalty with large groups of customers. What was historically commonplace in the village square marketplace can once again become the norm in large and small organisations.

Think FOR Your Customers does not mean you need to invest large amounts of money to change what you are doing. It does, however, mean changing your business culture and starting to think outside the box. But then, that has always been the fun of being in business!

Many of the examples given in this book are from the retail sector. However, all businesses have customers, clients, patients or visitors to their business or organisation, and the concepts used apply equally to all industries.

I hope you enjoy this book and find some ideas you can implement in your own business.

John Stanley

Changing the Face of Customer Service

As the world is changing, life is changing and customer service is changing. Failure to change could result in your business becoming an historical statistic.

You may believe that customer service has always been the same, and in some ways I agree. One of the first customer service experiences for mankind probably took place along the banks of the Euphrates River, near Babylon in Mesopotamia. Traders came from the east to sell spices, cloth, pottery and other products in the newly emerging civilisation. That was over five thousand years ago!

Take your mind back to what this experience was probably like. The ambience of the occasion would have stimulated all your senses. There would have been the aromas from all the spices, the sounds of musicians and people haggling and the whole experience of the market being a special space.

When it came to customer service, the traders probably didn't 'go for the jugular' and try and quickly close the sale. As a buyer, you'd have had a conversation about your life, their life, the local political scene, the weather, the upcoming sporting events and the origins and attributes of the product. Eventually, you'd make a decision on whether to purchase the product. Those eastern traders realised that making a sale was about social interaction. They realised that survival depended on their product and their personality and their ability to form a relationship with the potential customer. People purchased from traders they liked and trusted.

In 1786, Josiah Wedgwood, the British manufacturer of fine china, advertised in *The Times* newspaper for a shop

Memo

Many readers feel, quite rightly, that the world changed on September 11, 2001. But one of the most dramatic changes occurred with what is called 'Mead's Gap'. Mead's Gap occurred in 1957 with a generation of 'Sputnik Kids' who saw the first satellite go into space. It was the first generation of children who were exposed to a completely different world to the previous generation, literally overnight. This is when the 'generation gap' really started. That generation gap now occurs much more frequently – some say it occurs every six years.

It's become a real challenge to relate to all your customers in today's world.

manager, yet the advertisement mentioned he was looking for someone to *entertain* his customers.

So, whilst I agree that the basic rules of customer service have not changed, and that you and I are looking for social interaction and building relationships, in many ways customer service today is completely different from Mesopotamia. The means of transport then was a camel, it often took months for the trader and consumer to actually meet and trade was often via bartering. Consumers had to purchase perishables daily, and hygiene standards left a lot to be desired. Nevertheless, we still buy more from people we like and trust. That natural instinct was in us in ancient times and is still as strong in the 21st century. But how often do you, as a consumer, go to the shopping centre and find so-called 'salespeople' who don't realise that this is an integral part of their job description if the business is to prosper?

Compare the conditions in the ancient world to today, when you can switch on a computer in your own home and instantly purchase a product from a business halfway around the globe. What has happened in the intervening years is something Larry Downes and Chunka Mui call Killer Apps (*'Unleashing the Killer App'*, Harvard University Press). Killer Apps (or Killer Applications) are inventions that change the way we do things in business (and change our lives). Killer Apps include the wheel, stirrup, motorcar, electric light bulb, telephone, fax machine, computer and so on. These Killer Apps used to be sporadic but in the last few years we've had dozens a year. You may or may not be old enough to remember Yuri Gagarin's historic first flight into space, but have you ever considered that when you get in your car there are more computers hidden under the bonnet than were used in that journey?

This rapid change in technology has an inevitable impact on customer service in two ways.

Firstly it's having a huge impact on the way we do things. The computer is now an integral tool in the process of doing business and few people would go through a transaction where a computer wasn't used in some way. In fact you can easily complete a transaction and not have a human involved.

Secondly, all this technology makes a myth out of the concept that all customers are equal. Yes, we *were* all equal before these latest Killer Apps came along, but not any more. Because of computers and various software programs, businesses now know more about us as individuals than they have ever done before in the history of customer service.

Let me give you an instant example. This chapter is being constructed on a flight between Melbourne and Los Angeles — a dreaded fourteen-hour flight. The flight is completely full except for one empty seat. That seat is next to me. Why? Because on this flight, I'm the most frequent flyer. Frequent flyer's flight details are recorded in the airline company's computer. The airline's way of adding value to its customer service in this difficult situation is to take its most loyal passengers and provide them with the most comfort. It is adding value and, in a limited way, improving its most loyal customers' experience with this transaction.

There is an important key to this. Firstly, I (a loyal customer) am not complaining — in fact I'm delighted — but more importantly, modern technology means this favour the airline is doing for me is a secret between the flight attendant, myself, and you the reader. None of the other passengers, who are paying the same price as me, are aware why I have been given this favour of the empty seat next to me. Now that's an example of customer service in a changing world.

Modern technology allows you to segregate your customers, clients, patients or guests, (and I will use these descriptors interchangeably) based on gender, income, loyalty to your business, age group, interests and so on. You can now place a client in a category of one if you so wish.

From your customers' perspective, they now expect different service standards based on their individual needs. Elderly people expect a different service standard to a mother with young children. I know that many customers will tell you they should be treated equally, but don't believe them. Today everyone is special and because of the enabling technology customers now demand a service that's unique to them.

The big plus for this new technology is that it's readily available and cost-effective. The real challenge is finding the people to implement it effectively and with passion.

It's because of these sorts of changes that books like this go out of date quickly. Let's both be honest — the life of this book is a maximum of eighteen months. I'm suggesting that you take those customer service books off the shelf that were written last century (ie prior to four years ago) and trash them. They are out of date and old news. I'm not saying this out of arrogance, because I'm saying this book should also be trashed in eighteen months time, when it will also be out of date and old news. If it becomes your permanent customer service 'bible' then we both have a problem.

Memo

"When the rate of change outside your business is quicker than the rate of change inside your business, you have a short-lived business."

Jack Welch, CEO General Electric, USA

Don't let this state of affairs depress you. It's what makes customer service so exciting at present. It's a time of change and in times of change leaders emerge and show us the way forward. Your role is to be one of these leaders.

The Customer Is Always Right! Do You Think So?

Over my years as a consultant I've often heard the saying "the customer is always right". In almost every workshop and conference I do, one delegate is bound to mention it. Do you seriously believe this? I know I certainly don't. It may be something you feel should be said in customer service workshops, but in the real world this is a myth.

In his book 'At Your Service — Calamities, Catastrophes and other Curiosities of Customer Service' (John Wiley & Sons 1998, ISBN 0471255424), Hal Becker defines the real challenge we all have in business. He emphasises that the customer is often wrong, but that the customer is always in charge. This is the key to the challenge. If the customer feels he is not in charge, then he becomes someone else's customer.

We all provide customer service, but few of us get recognised for providing it. The reason for this is that all consumers have different definitions of what customer service is.

Ultimately, it's all down to values — not yours or mine — but the company's and how it delivers that to its customers. Every business has a culture and values, and its team members tend to perform to its lowest standards. The teams we respect work in businesses that have higher standards of culture and value than others that perform the same function in the marketplace. Businesses that write down their values and empower people to exceed those values are the ones you and I often have a higher respect for.

Company values will differ and definitions of customer service will also differ. One of my favourite definitions is from Canadian retailer and consultant Donald Cooper. He says that customer services are *"anything you do that in some small way reduces the stress of the customer"*. Companies that can identify what stresses their customers and then do something about it are heroes in their customers' eyes.

In *'Soul of the New Consumer — Authenticity, What We Buy and Why in the New Economy'* (Nicholas Brealey Publishing, 2000, ISBN 1-85788-246-6), authors David Lewis and Darren Bridger discuss what stresses customers. They researched shopping habits around the world and identified similar stress factors. In order of priority these were:

1. Congestion in streets and aisles
2. Delays — eg finding parking, queues at checkout
3. Difficulty locating items — they have moved, there is a lack of staff to ask, or a lack of staff with the relevant product knowledge
4. Loud music
5. Too hot/cold
6. Public address announcements
7. Lighting too bright/dim
8. Confusing store layout
9. Inefficient signage
10. Bad labelling

Donald Cooper operated a clothes shop in suburban Toronto and identified the changing room as one of the major stress factors in that industry. Once you've identified such a problem you can solve it, but alas, too many businesses simply ignore problems.

Ladies Changing Rooms – Look at the Opportunity

One of the biggest challenges for customers in many clothing stores is the changing room. The most important little room in the business is, in the customer's mind, often neglected.

As a consultant, one of the first rooms I check in a clothing store is the changing room. Sometimes it's cramped, dirty and hard to find, and sometimes it's at the other extreme and is so exposed that we can all see what's taking place inside.

Consumers often silently complain to themselves about the lack of hooks, chair, shelf, lighting, mirror and cleanliness and this can affect sales. Especially when you consider, for example, that only 25% of women in a jeans shop make a decision to purchase jeans *after* they have been in the changing rooms; the rest make the decision *in* the changing room (Ref: *'Why We Buy, The Science of Shopping'*, by Paco Underhill, Touchstone Books; June 2000, ISBN: 0684849143).

Doing business is about getting customers into your organisation and then converting them into purchasing a product or service. The major conversion actually takes place in the changing room — hence its importance. Business is also about image and your company image is reflected in the condition of your changing rooms. Many fashion stores fail to understand the importance of this room. The customer can often go from a highly professional business environment into a neglected part of the store. The objective is to provide an uplifting emotional experience, a place where your customers feel relaxed — the result will be a higher sales conversion rate.

Some stores over-emphasise what you can or cannot take into change rooms, giving the consumer the feeling that she is perceived as a thief. The "Alive and Well" store in Toronto, Canada had a policy that you could take as many items as you wished into the changing room and its customer conversion rate was one of the highest I have observed in Canada.

According to Jeffrey Kalinsky, owner of Canadian fashion store "Jeffrey", the basics of a dressing room should be a mirror, a seat and a carpet rug, as sweaty feet track dirt. Betty Halbreich, author of *'Confessions of a Retail Therapist'*, says that the ideal changing room must be spacious, private, furnished with two chairs, a small table, a high-quality mirror and at least three hooks.

Many consumers complain about lighting, which is why "Barneys" of New York has three settings for its changing room light switches; the settings are for day, office and evening. The Swedish retailer "Hand M" has signs in its changing rooms that say: "Would you like to change the light? If you press the button, the light will change to a colder daylight, which shows the colours of the garments in a more natural way". "The Banana Republic" flagship store in the USA also has what it calls 'Solstice Lighting' in its dressing rooms to let customers adjust the lights themselves to simulate day and night conditions.

Train the Team to be Consistent

Let us return to Hal Becker and his views on customer service. It's more than writing down your values and passing them on to new employees. As Hal suggests, there must be a non-stop training program. The format and style will vary dependant upon your business, but consistency will only be achieved by training the team in the same skills.

The only creature that can laugh is man; I believe that this must surely indicate that to get the best out of your team members, they must have fun. Your business's culture should make it a fun place to be for both your team and your customers. Don't develop a culture aimed solely at making customers happy — develop a culture to make team members happy. It's their job to then pass on their infectious positive attitude to your customers.

According to research carried out by Stamford University in the USA, the average person has around 60,000 thoughts a day, but 85% of these are negative. Eighty per cent of these negative thoughts are also 'leftover' thoughts from the previous day. Changing people's mindsets is the real challenge in sales and marketing.

"Pike's Fish Market" in Seattle, Washington is a glowing example of what can be done and how you can develop a positive culture in business. In 'Fish' (Hyperion, 2000, ISBN 0 340 82239 2), authors Stephen C Lundin, PhD, Harry Paul and John Christensen analyse the philosophy of Pike's and how it can be introduced into other businesses. The process is simplified into four steps:

Step 1: Start work with a positive attitude.

Step 2: Work must be fun.

Step 3: Make the customer's day.

Step 4: Show your customers that you're listening and that they have your undivided attention.

Have a Charter

In his book *'Success Through Excellence: How Companies in Australia are Seeking and Attaining Excellence'* (Beaumont Publishing House, 1992, ISBN 0646015079) Brett Whitford talks about companies having a customer service charter.

A charter is not a service guarantee; it is a minimum standard for the way a company performs in the eyes of its customers.

Charters will only work if the team believes in the company and its leader. I should correct that; charters only work if the team believes in the leader. Companies with the best leaders have the best customer service teams.

What company leaders do you admire and why? James Kouzes and Barry Posner have carried out extensive research on that subject and published it in *'The Leadership Challenge'* (Jossey-Bass Publishers, 3rd edition 2002, ISBN 0787956783). Their results show quite conclusively what people value in a company leader:

88% of people selected HONESTY

75% of people selected FORWARD-LOOKING

68% of people selected INSPIRING

63% of people selected COMPETENT

If you have those leadership talents, then introducing a customer service charter should be straightforward. The core values of that charter, according to Brett Whitford, should be:

Improve quality of service by continuous improvement

Provide honesty and integrity

Respect individuals

Value your customers

Instil in your team a sense of urgency regarding the need to provide positive experiences for customers

I have recently been working with a government organisation that's introducing change. It soon becomes evident in such a situation that one of the worst things you can do is create a committee. One committee took two years over making a decision on a team uniform and still could not come to an agreement! Instead, develop 'heroes' and give them deadlines. Those heroes may want to get a group together to discuss changes, but they have a commitment to a deadline. Customer service standards are changing too quickly for committees to ponder decisions.

Now is the time for action! Start making changes today!

Memo

Why do you choose to deal with one business over another business? It's not about price.

1. You LIKE the person – the INSTANT reaction

2. You TRUST the person – the LONG-TERM relation

Ref: Roy Brett Rutledge
Conference Speaker from New Zealand
brett@rutledge.co.nz

Think FOR Your Customers

Three Key Actions

- Identify what stresses your customers (that you have control over) and aim to reduce these stresses.
- Recruit people for personality; you're in the personality game. You can always train them in the relevant technical and knowledge skills.
- Start work with a positive attitude.

My Action Plan

1. _____

_____

_____

_____

_____

2. _____

_____

_____

_____

3. _____

_____

_____

_____

It's Time to Change the Culture

Sales are down, and more businesses like yours are competing in the marketplace. If this sounds familiar — what is the answer?

Far too many businesses choose to respond by reducing prices and, maybe, sending the team on a customer-care workshop. How often have businesses done this to find that turnover still keeps spiralling down?

Training team members in customer care is not the answer. It may, in fact, be detrimental to your business. It's not the team that needs to change — it's you!

Many team members I come across in my work know about and understand customer service, but fail to implement it because of the culture of the business, as they perceive it. The first major challenge is to change the culture of the business, not to change the team. The first question that needs to be answered is why there's a culture problem in the first place. Not many business owners realise that this is the key.

One part of the problem is that most business owners get locked into day-to-day survival mode and they fail to see the 'big picture' of what is happening in the business, and how it is affecting the bottom line. The result is that everyone's busy doing things but failing to grow their businesses through their team members.

Every business has a culture: it's how you change the culture to be more positive that is the real key to success.

I recently worked with a business owner who had set up his business from nothing ten years ago and who now employed a team of 50 people. The business had initially grown rapidly and the owner was still developing ideas to continue to grow the business. He was, however, showing signs of burnout and the business's growth had stagnated.

During the consulting session this businessman came up with at least a dozen ideas on how to grow his business. Finally, I stopped him and asked him how many ideas his team had come up with over the last month. His reply was "none". When I asked about the previous month, the answer was still "none". What amazed me was that 50 team members had produced no ideas to share on how to grow the business in the last two months. What amazed him was that I thought that they *should* have had ideas. He pointed out to me that it was his business and not their business. He had never asked his team for ideas.

This is a prime example of where a cultural change is essential if a business is to develop, mature, and prosper. Leave all the thinking to one person and you'll never get all the ideas you need to grow a business in a changing world. Share the idea creation amongst a team and you will get a 'team-load' of ideas. Your only challenge will be managing the changes based on these ideas.

Empowerment

Before you start *Thinking FOR Your Customers* you have to get your team to think FOR your customers. The answer is not for you to do the thinking, but for the team to do the thinking. As a manager you need to empower the team members to enable them to have the confidence to think for your customers.

Memo

Customer Service Is On the Slide

According to the Customer Satisfaction Ratings in the USA, customers believe service standards are dropping.

Look at the following results:

1994 – 2000	
Computer companies	- 5%
Airlines	- 12%
Retail	- 3.7%
Hotels	- 4.7%
US Postal Service	+ 4%
South West Airlines	- 10.3%
Dell Computers	+ 11.1%
Compaq	- 9.0%
K-Mart	- 9.5%
Volkswagen	+ 12.2%

Are we, as customers, expecting more, or are standards dropping? That's the challenge.

Ref: Steve Simpson, 'UGR's Cracking the Corporate Culture Code', Narnia House Publishing, 2001, Western Australia, ISBN 0-9579316-0-3

To achieve this you may need to make some attitudinal changes in your business. Ask yourself these important questions:

1. If a stranger approached any of your team members and asked them what the growth plans were for your business over the next three years, would they be able to tell him?

2. If that same stranger asked them what your company believed in when it came to customer service, would they be able to answer, and would all the team provide a consistent answer?

3. How many new ideas has each team member contributed to the pool of ideas in your business over the last month?

4. What rewards system is in place for team members who provide great ideas?

5. Does each team member have a job description that is measurable? Do you monitor this on a regular basis (ie at least twice a year)?

For people to grow they need a vision. Keep the team in the dark and they will react accordingly. You need to provide customer service that inspires and is memorable. To achieve this you need a team that is inspired. Not everyone has to agree with your company dreams and goals. But, if you don't share your vision with the team, they will not grow and will just 'do the job'.

Prepare a portfolio on your business goals and dreams. Get the team together and share these goals and dreams. Put a deadline on the dreams, so the team members are aware that they are actual (probably long-term) goals rather than unobtainable dreams.

Create a sharing culture. I'm a believer in the maxim that the biggest threat to a business is a boss with an idea! I come across too many businesses where the boss is the one who has the ideas and the team members therefore don't share their ideas with the boss, even though their ideas are realistic, practical and could improve the bottom line.

Once a month, have a brainstorming session, but one in which the boss must not contribute a single idea. Encourage the team to come up with the ideas — be a facilitator. If you can create a culture where the team provides ideas to develop customer service, you'll be amazed how rapidly things will change in your business!

We All Need Heroes

I firmly believe that we all need heroes. Your business needs heroes. You need a hero that you can measure your business by. Who are the business leaders you admire? Are you modelling yourself on them? When you have exceeded your heroes' standards in the way they exceed their customers' expectations, then you're really *Thinking FOR Your Customers.*

Thinking FOR Your Customers is a journey that will never end, as once you've started thinking for your customers you will constantly be challenging yourself and your team to exceed your customers' expectations and always to provide the unexpected extra service.

Walk the Customer's Journey

A customer plans to visit your establishment for the first time. This is a critical time for you, as he is about to make decisions that will reflect on your relationship with him for many visits to come.

You need to 'change shoes' at least once a week and walk the same journey as your customers, to ensure their journey is a memorable and positive experience.

This journey can be split into three very specific physical zones:

IMAGE ZONE
(How they view your business)

TRANSITION ZONE
(How they perceive your business when they enter it)

EXCITEMENT / PRODUCT ZONE
(How they are stimulated by what you offer)

These three zones will be experienced by your customers in less than 10 seconds, but are critical in developing a positive relationship with them.

The image zone starts outside your business. Your adverts, external landscaping, paint work and shop window displays are all going to play an integral part in creating a mental picture of what the customer is going to expect from the whole experience he will have within your business.

For example, I recently worked with a public library. All the team members came to work via the 'back' door. As a consultant, I entered via the front door. My visit was ten days after a national holiday on which all businesses were closed. As I entered, there was a large sign across the front door informing everyone that the library would be closed next Thursday for the holiday. When I pointed out that the holiday was the previous week, it became clear that nobody in the library was walking the building as a customer. They were all entering by the wrong door!

Image can change by the moment. Litter on the floor or dirty fingerprints on windows can change your image in just seconds. It's essential that all your team members are aware of how important the 'image zone' is and that they are empowered to take appropriate action to correct any flaw in the image immediately.

The 'transition zone' in an establishment is usually the first three steps that a potential visitor takes once he has crossed the threshold. He doesn't concentrate on products or signs in this zone; he is taking in the whole environment. Keep this zone uncluttered, clean and inviting.

Finally, customers focus on what I call the power position, which is the excitement/product zone. This is a focal point directly in front of them as they pass through the transition zone. This point should clearly state what you do and it should stimulate the visitor's interest. Keep it simple; create circular, conical displays that promote key issues about your business. Dare to be different in how you get this message across!

These three zones are the most memorable part of the customer's journey! This experience is often called 'The Moment of Truth'. A customer may spend 20 minutes, or more, in your business, but take home a picture based on a maximum of (the initial) 30 seconds spent in your establishment.

I'm a great believer in image checklists that can be used in the business on a daily basis. The checklist opposite is provided as an idea, which you may need to adapt for your own business.

EXAMPLE

Daily Checklist

	completed (Tick ✓) Signature
1. Out of date material removed from counter	
2. Brochure holders full of relevant leaflets	
3. Velcro, Blu-Tack and sticky tape removed	
4. Windows and doors clean (no fingerprints)	
5. Time on clock is correct	
6. Rubbish bins emptied	
7. Everyone is wearing the corporate uniform and name badges	
8. Any clutter removed from counter	
9. Floors clean and all litter removed	
10. Restocking of 'impulse' displays completed	
11. All potential hazards removed eg scissors, etc.	
12. All lights are working	
13. All signage is relevant to today	
14. Fill 'power displays' with key product	
15. All faded, ripped signs removed	

Create an Experience

Everyone wants an experience when he or she deals with a business, but do you provide a memorable one?

There is an excellent book, *'The Experience Economy: Work is Theatre and Every Business a Stage'* by B. Joseph Pine II and James H. Gilmore (HBS Press, Boston, Mass. 1999, ISBN 0-87584-819-2) that challenges the way you think about creating the right experience for your customers in your business.

How do you create the best experience? Well, firstly you have to accept that customers look for experiences, not just products or services. This means we must engage with each visitor to our establishment if we are to create a positive, memorable experience that will enable us to build a relationship in which we can better fulfil their needs.

Pine and Gilmore talk about the importance of 'the experience wheel' and illustrate what you can do to enhance the customer's experience.

Experience enhancement covers four areas of your business:
Entertainment
Education
Escapism
Aesthetics

Entertainment

Many business owners believe that if they introduce Disney-style entertainment they are creating an experience for the customer. An experience is more than entertainment. Yes, you need to provide unique entertainment, but remember that's only a quarter of the experience package that you need to apply in your business.

Education

Customers like to learn whilst on the journey with your business. If you want to enhance the experience, you need to apply an education package to the product mix.

This may take a number of forms:

- Product signage on origin of product, artist involved or how it was used in ancient times.
- Workshops that you conduct in your business. 'How to' workshops providing customers with new skills can be exceptionally valuable.
- Train the team to be storytellers rather than product sellers.

Escapism

Do you have the opportunity in your business to get customers really involved? If they are doing things, they are experiencing things. This may take the form of a climbing wall in a sports shop, a planting station in a garden centre, or a massage in a health shop. The list is endless, but it needs you and your team to brainstorm what *you* can do in *your* business.

Memo

"Be outrageous, it's the only place that ain't crowded."

Ref. Janet Knapp, conference speaker at ANLA Conference, 2003.

Aesthetics

Engage all the senses. Are your customers hearing the right music, smelling the right aroma, and do you have an opportunity to include taste testing? Those retailers who put up signs that read "Please don't touch" have a long way to go to get into 'the experience economy'.

Think FOR Your Customer

Three Key Actions

- Encourage each team member to provide at least one idea a month on how to improve the business.
- Empower team members to make decisions with their customers.
- Create an image checklist and use it every day.

My Action Plan

1. _____

   _____

   _____

   _____

2. _____

   _____

   _____

   _____

3. _____

   _____

   _____

   _____

SECTION 2

Understanding the Selling Process

The process of selling is a simple one, but is often misunderstood by many businesses.

Firstly, let's go through the whole process. Not everyone walking past your business is intending to be a customer of yours. I believe that if you analysed your passing traffic you could divide people into one of six categories. How you then view those categories influences the way you market your business.

Memo

But All People Want Is Price!

How often have you heard salespeople say that the biggest issue for their customers is price? Yet all the research shows that price is the third or fourth consideration in the customer's mind. The comments from salespeople don't match the research. What's happening out in the marketplace?

Barry Urquhart addresses this issue in his book 'Marketing Magic', (Marketing Focus, Western Australia, 2001, ISBN 0-9586558-20). What he has found is that if the customer does not have confidence in the salesperson, then price becomes more of an issue than it would otherwise have been. Back to trust! Consumer price sensitivity is closely related to team member confidence. Confident team members will grow your business.

Some of those passers-by will be **suspects.** These are people who are suspicious of what you do and have no intention of dealing with your business. If you promote yourself to these people you're wasting money, time and effort. For example, you may have a butcher shop and some of your passers-by may be vegetarians; or a golf shop and some passers-by may hate sport. Don't spend time, effort and money trying to convert these passers-by into your customers — they don't want to play the game!

Other people walking past your door will be **prospects.** These people may enter your establishment if you invite them in. At present they have no intention of entering because you haven't provided them with a strong enough reason to venture in. These people are an opportunity to grow your customer base.

The third group of people are **shoppers.** They purchase what you sell, but don't purchase it from your establishment. Again, they need an incentive to change their shopping habits and enter your business, rather than shop at your competition's business.

The next group are **customers.** They actually enter your establishment, but also go elsewhere to check out the range on offer and buy from your competition.

They may also spread their shopping amongst several stores like your own. They are not loyal to you, probably because you've never asked them to become loyal patrons.

The next group are your **clients.** These customers are loyal to you but don't promote you via word of mouth to their friends or colleagues. The irony is that if you provided an incentive for them to do so, they would actually gladly do it. This could be the most cost-effective way of growing your business.

The final group are your **advocates.** They are 100% loyal and always promote your establishment by word of mouth, without being asked to. They are also very professional at doing it, using words like:

"I'll introduce you to *my* hairdresser."

"*My* butcher is excellent."

"Next time you go on holiday use *my* travel agent and mention *my* name."

As you can see, the '*my*' word is very important. They will put their reputations at stake to promote your business and will do it without being paid to do so!

Therefore, to start the selling process face-to-face, you have to consider what is the most effective way of getting these groups of people through your door.

Well, firstly, forget the suspects — you won't get rich trying to get these guys into your business. The key is to concentrate on the other categories.

Interruption Marketing versus Permission Marketing

There are basically two techniques you can use to attract these passers-by.

You have to interrupt the thought processes of prospects, shoppers and some customers. You are not a priority in their minds and you need to get your name and product into their minds. You literally have to interrupt their thinking processes. As you'd expect, this can be expensive and may not work, as others are also trying to interrupt their thought processes. You need to get people to think of your organisation *first* when they are considering how to fulfil their needs. You need a share of their minds, not a share of the market, with these target groups.

Examples of interruption marketing are television commercials, newspaper advertising, mail-outs, billboards, promotional signage and radio adverts. Think about it — you and I are exposed to thousands of advertising interruptions every day. How many do we, firstly, remember and secondly, act upon? Very few. This is why interruption marketing is expensive; it's basically ineffective, but it's an essential tool nonetheless.

Customers, clients and advocates can be exposed to permission marketing. This is where you invest in targeted marketing to members of a market sector that has given you permission to market to them, with the aim of building their loyalty. The most common example of permission marketing is the use of loyalty clubs and loyalty cards (Note: a discount card is not a loyalty card!).

We need to understand the above strategies prior to looking at the selling formulae. Companies have to invest in getting customers to the door. Alas, the majority of them don't come for free.

The Selling Formulae

LEADS GENERATED   You need to invest in interruption marketing to generate leads.

Once the potential customers have reached your premises you now have to rely on company representatives to convert them into customers.

CONVERSION   You need an investment in recruitment and training to ensure you have the best ambassador for your business.

The investment in marketing, recruitment and training should produce a new customer from each lead.

Formula 1: LEADS GENERATION x CONVERSION = NEW CUSTOMER

That is the start of the selling process, or should be. Alas, in many businesses it's the start and the finish.

The next stage is to add your new customers to your existing customers.

EXISTING CUSTOMERS You need an investment in permission marketing.

Formula 2: NEW CUSTOMERS + EXISTING CUSTOMERS = NUMBER OF CUSTOMERS A YEAR

If you multiply this by:

FREQUENCY OF VISITS   An investment in training to ensure your team have the skills to build loyalty.

then you'll have the total number of transactions in your business during, for example, a twelve-month period. We can now turn this into a monetary equation simply by multiplying this by the average spending per customer.

AVERAGE TRANSACTION   An investment in training in product knowledge and communication skills will increase this figure.

The resultant figure is the expected income from your business over a twelve-month period.

LEADS GENERATED x CONVERSION = NEW CUSTOMER

NEW CUSTOMERS + EXISTING CUSTOMERS = ANNUAL CUSTOMER COUNT

Formula 3: CUSTOMER COUNT x FREQUENCY OF VISITS x AVERAGE TRANSACTION = TOTAL INCOME FROM SALES

As you can see from this equation, a number of people in the organisation have a key role in customer service and these people need to be communicating a consistent message. Investment should be focused on increasing all of the above factors. A small increase in each of the above makes a big difference to your business.

Let me give you an example:

Leads Generated	x Conversions	= new Customers	+ Existing customers	= total Customers	X Frequency a year	x Average sale	= Yearly sales
100	50%	50	50	100	5	10	5000
110	55%	55	55	110	6	12	7920

Let me explain this chart. Don't concentrate all your efforts on improving one area of your business. Concentrate on the whole process and aim at small improvements.

In the example I have given, if you attract 10% more customer leads and convert half of them, as well as getting all your customers to come one more time a year and spend an extra 20%, then your sales can go up by over 50%.

It's the little differences that produce the biggest results.

To improve your customer service you need to look at the full customer picture. Your objective is to increase their lifetime value with your business. Most businesses look to keep loyal customers as lifetime customers for about ten years.

I'm a firm believer that everyone in your team should know the lifetime monetary value of his customers. Why? It will make him view those customers in a completely different light.

Again, let me give you an example.

I may visit the same delicatessen every working day, but I may only spend $5 on each visit. If the sales team members haven't been initiated in lifetime values then they will just regard me as a '$5 customer' and will subsequently treat me accordingly.

However, if they understand lifetime values, then the story changes dramatically.

$5 customer comes five times a week	=	$25.00
Visit deli for 50 weeks a year	=	$1,250.00
Shops at deli for 10 years	=	$12,500.00

Our $5 customer's lifetime value actually brings in $12,500 to our business. If the team members know that I'm sure they will treat the customer in a completely different way.

Remember, as far as the customer is concerned, his customer-care experience starts at home with his anticipation and expectations, develops inside your premises, and finishes when he puts the product away after he has returned home. It's your job to make the total experience an enjoyable one, not just the experience within the four walls of your business.

For example: it's time to do the weekly grocery shopping. Your consumer makes a list by looking in the pantry and fridge, then gets in the car and gets frustrated trying to find a parking space. He does the shopping and has to line up at the checkout for 15 minutes. Finally the customer gets served and hauls five bags of goods to the car. He gets home and unpacks to find the tomatoes squashed at the bottom of the bag and that the washing powder has been forgotten.

You may have provided excellent customer service in the supermarket, but the customer's perception of the experience is a negative one. Customer service is more than smiles in the supermarket, it's about a total service that starts and finishes at the customer's home or office.

It's More Than Customer Service

I'm fully aware that the above formulae involve more than investment in customer service. For example, your average sale is strongly influenced by your product mix, traffic flow, price and signage strategies, and merchandise positioning. Nevertheless, the driving force is still primarily customer service and it is these skills I wish to develop within this book. It's a simple rule: products don't sell — people sell.

Emotional Marketing

Customer loyalty is one of the major keys to success. Some companies excel at building loyalty — others have not yet discovered the magical secret of loyal customers.

When it comes to working with customers' emotions one of the master businesses is "Hallmark Cards". Scott Robinette, Clare Brand and Vicki Leng discuss this in depth in their book *'Emotion Marketing: The Hallmark Way of Winning Customers for Life'* (McGraw-Hill Trade, 2000, ISBN: 0071364145). As we are all aware, Hallmark markets to the customer's heart.

Your aim is to move the customers from satisfaction to loyalty and the magic ingredient is emotion. There has to be an emotional link. What does Hallmark do? It shows people it cares, and alas in a recent survey in the USA only 4% of shoppers felt that businesses they dealt with were 'caring' companies. Hallmark has an emotional marketing plan that it calls 'Value Star', based on five key points: Equity, Experience, Energy, Product and Money.

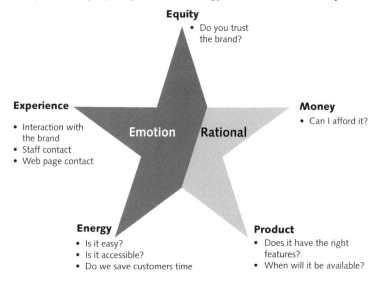

Equity
• Do you trust the brand?

Experience
• Interaction with the brand
• Staff contact
• Web page contact

Emotion   **Rational**

Money
• Can I afford it?

Energy
• Is it easy?
• Is it accessible?
• Do we save customers time

Product
• Does it have the right features?
• When will it be available?

Ref: *'Emotional Marketing: The Hallmark Way of Winning Customer for Life'.*

All points of the Hallmark Value Star are equal, and the last thing you can afford is a negative prong to the Star's points.

"When you care enough to send the very best."

Hallmark's recognised slogan is a real challenge to any business. It works for Hallmark, but could it work for your business? Could your business alter it to say:

"When you care enough to buy the best groceries."
"..use the best kitchen designers."
"..seek the best advice."

(How would you finish this sentence in your organisation?)

When you know you can deliver it, then you know you have a winning formula. It's not based on the rational elements of your business. It's based on 'the three E's' of Equity, Experience and Energy.

Does the Team Know its Role?

Basically, selling is about being an effective host, consultant, and seller. A professional salesperson knows the process and knows how to implement the process.

Remember — personality sells. The last thing I'm advocating is a scripted sales pitch — something that throws personality out of the game plan straight away. What your team needs is a process. The roles of the participants are shown in the table overleaf:

Don't assume anything in customer care. Have a policy and ensure everyone understands his or her role in the customer care game.

Memo

Maybe Your Suppliers Have to Think FOR Your Customers

A client of mine is a major supplier to businesses around the world. This client was finding that it had a superb product, but market penetration was not as effective as it should be.

When the client's management asked the businesses it supplied for ideas, none were forthcoming, as the businesses were happy with the category performance.

It was time to talk to the real experts, the consumer and the end user. What did they tell the supplier?

(1) You use industry technology we do not understand and we are embarrassed to ask for it to be explained to us.

(2) The company offers too much choice within a range and this confuses us. We don't know what products the company really believes in.

(3) The way the category is laid out confuses us and it is difficult to select products.

(4) There are no helpful shelf talkers to help us select the right product at the right time.

When these concerns were addressed and new category layouts were implemented, sales increased by 40%.

Is your merchandise strategy confusing your customers and limiting your sales?

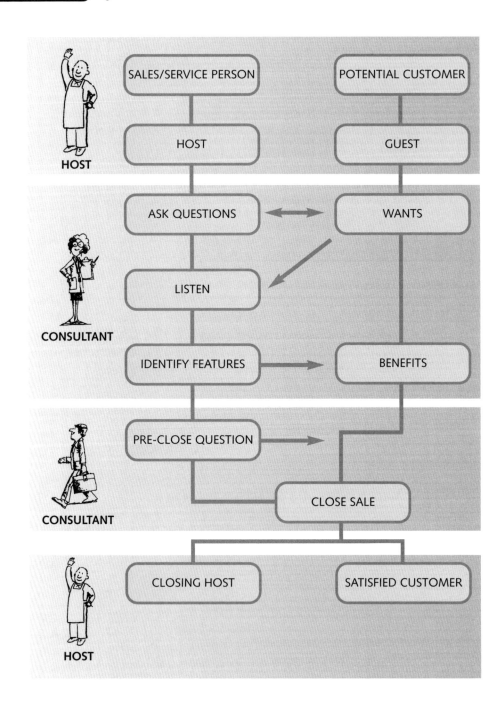

Research carried out by Carole Walker, director of "Service Audits and Market Research", Western Australia, indicates that consumers in shopping centres are doing less browse-shopping and therefore organisations need to be more pro-active to gain customer confidence.

Carole Walker specialises in customer service 'benchmarking' of retailers.

She surveys customers to ask what their expectations are and uses these as a benchmark for retailers. Her research covers various retail sectors and allows a company to benchmark itself against a consumer's standard.

Her overall figures are showing the following results:

98% of customers expect the respondent to speak clearly and adopt a positive tone of voice.

92% of customers expect that the store name will be clearly stated.

92% of customers expect that the information provided by the respondent is both informative and relevant to their inquiry.

90% of customers expect to be offered a greeting.

90% of customers expect to be asked appropriate questions to establish the reason for their call.

84% of customers expect to be thanked for calling the business.

75% of customers expect that a business phone will be answered within three rings.

65% of customers expect that the name of the team member responding to the call will be provided.

48% of customers expect to be invited into the store as a means of offering further assistance.

44% of customers expect the respondent to wait for them to disconnect the call first.

This is what consumers expect, but how often it's provided is another matter.

Compare your service against what other companies are doing, both inside and outside of your industry sector.

I recently worked with a hardware chain that was comparing its customer service to other hardware retailers and was confident it was out-servicing its competition. What it had not done was to compare its customer service standards against other businesses that the consumer visits.

The consumer under consideration was not shopping in different hardware stores; rather he was using this store and comparing service with the newsagent, grocery store, hairdresser and library. These businesses were the ones who should have been used in the benchmarking comparison.

Think FOR Your Customer

Three Key Actions

- Change customer thinking from 'THE' to 'MY'.
- Ensure all your team members know the average sale per customer.
- Ensure all the team members know the lifetime value of your average customer.

My Action Plan

1. _____

_____

_____

_____

2. _____

_____

_____

_____

3. _____

_____

_____

_____

SECTION 3

How to Become an Effective Host

– *Your Moment of Truth*

Ten seconds is not long enough, but that is all you are given to make a first impression on visitors to your organisation. The term 'moment of truth' was coined by Jan Carlzon, the director of Scandinavian Airlines, in his book *'Moments of Truth — New Strategies for Today's Customer Driven Economy'*, (Ballinger Publishing, 1987, ISBN 0-06-091580-3).

What it means, basically, is that customers judge people and businesses in the first ten seconds. If they feel positive and like the person or business in these first ten seconds then the chances are a positive relationship will follow. If they feel negative about the moment, then the chances are you will not build the rapport with the customer that is necessary in order to grow the relationship.

The moment of truth is under your control, as the host or salesperson, and therefore we need to analyse what you can do to make this a pleasant experience.

In such a short time the potential customer is not going to take in what you say. How often have you been introduced to somebody and forgotten his name instantly? The reason for this is that you are absorbing other signals from this stranger you've just met.

In the first ten seconds we can divide up your reading of the person as follows.

Body Language

The most important part of the first ten seconds is how we read people's body language. It's not so much what we say, it's the way that we say it that is important.

TONE / ACCENT 10%

BODY LANGUAGE 70%

APPEARANCE 20%

Many books have been written on body language over the years and if you wish to delve into this fascinating subject more deeply, then you should obtain a good book on the subject. I recommend Allan Pease's *'Signals — How to Use Body Language for Power, Success, and Love'* (Bantam Books; Re-issue edition (August 1, 1984), ISBN: 0553343661).

I cannot emphasise enough how important it is that your team members are aware of how critical it is to get the body language right when meeting customers. We can either send out positive or negative messages based on how we stand, sit or present ourselves. Remember — it's what the receiver reads in our body language that is important.

The table below indicates the main signals we send out as positive or negative messages.

Body Language Clues — Facing Gestures

Positive gestures ☺	Negative gestures ☹
Eye contact	No eye contact Look down Look at the ceiling Wearing sunglasses so that the customer cannot read your eyes
Smile	**Frown**
Hands kept clear of the face	Stroking a beard Fiddling with long hair Rubbing one's ear Stroking the side of the nose

We normally send these messages out subconsciously, which makes it a lot more difficult to control and measure.

The above examples are based on Caucasian habits and perceptions. Culturally, people of many cultures will not make eye contact when they meet people. If, for example, you meet an indigenous Australian, a Japanese person or a South African Zulu, you will notice that out of politeness in their culture they will not make eye contact when they greet you.

Body Language Clues — Standing Up

Positive gestures ☺	Negative gestures ☹
Open hand gestures Talking with the hands	Arms folded. *This is putting a wall up between you and the person you're talking to.*
Facing the customer/client squarely	Crossing your legs away from the person. *The leading foot is often facing your escape route.*

Body Space

The distance between people when they are standing up is a fascinating subject. Women tend to want about a third more space than men do, whilst holding a conversation when standing.

The comfort distance between us depends again on our culture and where we live as well as on individual psychology. The largest space between people occurs in rural communities in Australia, whilst some of the closest 'people-space' zones can be found in Indonesia. The British need a larger personal space than the French; Australians need more space than New Zealanders do, and so it varies between cultures. Getting personal space right is a real challenge in a multicultural business world.

Body Language Clues — Sitting Down

Positive gestures ☺	Negative gestures ☹
Facing the person squarely	Sitting with your legs crossed away from the person you're talking to.

It's amazing how conversations can change, based on how seating positions are arranged. If your aim is to have an open conversation, then the seating arrangements is critical to your success.

Eg. Formal seating arrangements (less relaxed conversation

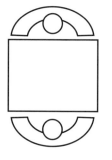

Informal seating
arrangements
(more open conversation)

The 'moment of truth' can set the agenda for an hour-long meeting. It is critical that you get it right otherwise the 'tone' of the meeting can be influenced. This would affect anything from the average sale per customer to the outcome of a detailed financial agreement.

Memo

Children laugh 600 times a day.

Adults laugh 20 times a day.

Retailing should be fun – laugh more often.

Tone / Accent

People don't listen to words straight away. Initially, they react to a tone and/or accent. They need to read from that tone whether they are in for a positive or negative experience. Based on the tone, they will subconsciously decide on how to react to you.

Smiling people tend to have a more pleasant tone than people who frown, so the key is to smile prior to opening your mouth. Especially when you consider it only takes three muscles to smile, compared to 40 muscles to frown.

How often have you painted a picture in your mind's eye of a person, when all you have is an audio message from him or her? The majority of us paint an attractive person if the tone is pleasant and the reverse if the tone is perceived as unpleasant.

Appearance

Yes, people do put us in 'boxes' based on what we wear. Even in these more liberal times there are dress codes that customers and clients expect us to adhere to. Assume you'd never met your bank manager and you were called into a meeting. On meeting you, the bank manager was in his office wearing sandals, Bermuda shorts and a 'kiss-me-quick' T-shirt. Your initial response would probably be not to trust the banking advice you were about to be offered. Dressing down is now fashionable, but you can take this too far and lose credibility. Getting the balance right is crucial.

Many companies have a corporate uniform or a written dress code. Personally, I am a great believer in this approach. I don't believe you can afford to put the image of your company in the hands of an individual's whims and fashion statements.

Consistency is the name of the game. Once you have appearance rules laid down in your organisation, everyone must adhere to them. You cannot afford a 'prima donna' who feels he or she is above company rules and policies. Not only does this confuse the customer, but it also undermines your management style in the eyes of the team.

When it comes to appearance, there are some further thoughts I would like to share.

* In friendly companies, name badges should be essential. Use first names only and put the name in lower case eg 'John'. You don't need to provide positions or titles, as the customer isn't interested. Make the print large enough so the customer can read it without getting embarrassed. If, for example, you have two 'Johns' in your team, then give one of them a stage name (it could be his middle name), as this will prevent customer confusion.

  I always remember a company that had two 'Susans' on the team. A customer had dealt with one Susan and had returned for further assistance. The customer met the manager and asked for Susan. When the manager asked "Which one?" the customer replied "The good looking one!" The message is simple — don't get yourself into a similarly embarrassing position.

  Always get two badges made for each member of your team. Give one badge to the team member and keep one in the office. Sooner or later someone is going to leave a badge at home. When that occurs, he or she can obtain one from the office by donating a pre-defined and agreed amount to a company charity. In my experience this works exceptionally well.

* In some industries, young people often don't 'look the part' due to their age. How often have you heard customers whispering that "he doesn't look old enough..." to do whatever task he is involved in? We older members of the work force believe some policemen don't look old enough to do their jobs these days.

  To help credibility in this situation, provide 'tools of the trade' to younger team members. The tools will vary, depending on what job they are involved in, but could include secateurs (garden centre), tape measure (tailor) back brace (hardware), and so on.

- Uniforms are for work and to provide a professional image. It would be flattering if your uniform were so fashionable that team members wanted to wear it in their social time, but I would have a policy in which they cannot wear it outside work. You have no control over team members' social life, nor should you. But the last thing you want is someone getting drunk with, or being seen by, potential customers whilst he is still wearing your company's staff uniform. This is not going to enhance your business image.

- There is more to it than uniform. You may have to stipulate conditions on hairstyle, cosmetics and jewellery. This may be due to safety reasons, or based on consumers' expectations. Team members have to relate to consumers and what is acceptable as a fashion statement to an 18-year-old may not be acceptable to someone in his late fifties. It's the customers your team members have to relate to, not only their peers.

- In most businesses, smoking at work is now unacceptable. People are asked to smoke outside the workplace. I don't want to get into the pros and cons of smoking, but I would have a policy that people can't smoke at the front entrance of your business.

  I recently worked for a supermarket where smoking on the premises was banned. At certain times of the day, customers had to fight their way through a group of smokers outside the front entrance to get into the establishment. Again, this is not giving customers a positive moment of truth.

Make sure all your team members are aware of the skills required to make a positive first impression.

You don't get a second chance to make a first impression.

Think FOR Your Customer

Three Key Actions

- Review your dress code and ensure everyone looks professional.
- Ensure everyone knows the rules when they play the body language game.
- Make sure the team members are aware of cultural differences when they play the game.

My Action Plan

1. _____

    _____

    _____

    _____

    _____

2. _____

    _____

    _____

    _____

3. _____

    _____

    _____

    _____

SECTION 4

How to Become an Effective Consultant
– Talk to Me and Build a Relationship

In my conference presentations, I often talk about the importance of personality when building a relationship with a customer. I stress that you recruit for personality and you then train the team in technical knowledge.

Often I get a strange look, as many businesses still believe the key to success is technical knowledge. It still surprises me that some industries continue to over-emphasise this in their pre-industry training.

Memo

Successful salespeople:
They love to make sales.
They respect their customers.

Ref: Cathcart, Jim. 'Relationship Selling: The key to getting and keeping customers'. Perigee Book, The Berkley Publishing Group, New York, 1990. ISBN-0-399-51644-1.

I recently met a librarian who had just finished her degree. She had spent a number of years at a university, studying the technical aspects of being a librarian. For me, some of the key areas of customer service include knowing how to merchandise, display, and build relationships, but none of this was even discussed in her course.

Work carried out in the 1980s by the Carnegie Foundation in the USA, and reported in Jim Cathcart's book, 'Relationship Selling: the key to getting and keeping customers', determined that a person's success was based 15% on technical knowledge and 85% on his ability to manage himself in the situation. Personality played a key role in this process.

Play with a Boomerang

In Australia, one of our unofficial national symbols is a boomerang — a kind of throwing weapon invented by our indigenous people. Throw a boomerang and, with skill (a lot of skill), it will return to you.

Thinking FOR a customer encompasses some of the principles of throwing a boomerang. Your aim should be to ensure that the customer comes back to you on a regular basis. You want 'boomerang customers'.

We have dealt with the same travel agent for a number of years and have stayed loyal, due to his implementation of the boomerang principle.

At regular intervals he notifies us of special deals or packages in travel that may help our business. He is not in the business of selling us our tickets; he is in the business of reducing our stress when we travel.

Whether you're a librarian, bank teller, travel agent, greengrocer, general retailer, or other organisation, the boomerang principle always works in the long run.

Sales people need a happy people-oriented personality to do the job well. This is more important now than it's ever been. Look at what you sell and check whom else sells it. I recently worked with a small delicatessen in a medium-sized town. It sold bananas, amongst other products. When I asked the owners why people came to their deli, I was told it was because they sold bananas and other products that people wanted. I then asked them where else I could purchase bananas within the catchment area. They estimated that there were about 12 other outlets nearby where customers could buy bananas. It is not the product that is the reason that people come to an establishment; every one of those other 12 outlets sold the same quality product. People come to your establishment because of you! You make the point of difference that customers judge your business on.

> **Memo**
>
> The three main reasons people buy:
> They TRUST the seller.
> They LIKE the product.
> They FEEL the product is worth the price.
>
> Ref: Relationship Selling

Therefore, your skills, your approach, your attitude, your knowledge, your empathy and your communication skills are your point of difference. If you don't have the necessary relationship skills, your business will not prosper.

In this section of the book, I want to concentrate on how you can build a relationship with your customers based on your verbal communications. Remember: this is only one part of the relationship equation, but it is a critical part.

Can I Help? Are You All Right?

The purpose of initiating a sales relationship is to open a conversation, identify your client's needs and wants, build a relationship with your client and thereby increase your average sale.

What's the most difficult way of achieving the above? By using a closed question such as *"Can I help you?"* or *"Are you all right?"* What is a customer's natural response to a closed question? Without even thinking about it, a customer will respond on most occasions with, *"No, thanks, just looking"* or *"I'm fine thanks"*. The conversation is then closed down permanently.

Customers tend to close down the conversation when approached by a team member who asks a closed question. These customers probably think that the person doesn't really want to get involved anyway. The customer's perception may be 'why waste time?' when the salesperson seems unable to relate to him when greeting him.

Researchers tell us that 70% of customers close down a conversation that starts with a closed question. In other words, we carry on playing the game by the same rules.

Rather than criticise the user of the closed question, we should analyse why this is taking place. What the customer identifies is a symptom — what we need to discover and remedy is the cause.

Memo

The six main reasons people don't buy:

1. WRONG seller.
2. WRONG product.
3. WRONG price.
4. WRONG time.
5. WRONG sales technique.
6. Because they were never asked!

Ref: Relationship Selling.

Why do professional salespeople use closed questions? I believe there are two major reasons:

- They see the owner using closed questions and therefore they copy the owner's example and thus perform to the lowest accepted standard of the business.

  The owner or manager's role in the business is not to sell; it is to operate a profitable business. How often have you seen an owner walk across a shop floor with plenty of tasks on his mind? Halfway across the shop floor he sees a customer seeking help. His natural reaction is to respond to the immediate situation. He approaches the customer, wanting to help but not wanting to get involved. A *"Can I help you?"* comes out without even thinking about it. The customer says *"No thank you"* and the owner carries on thinking about the tasks that he has in his mind.

Often, the worst role model you can have for a salesperson is the owner. This is not a criticism of owners. Owners should be role models for leaders, not salespeople. But, when they do become sales role models, it has to be because they can achieve exceptionally high levels of relationship building and sales. Their teams will copy them and use them as models for their minimum standard.

- Think back to what you were like as a typical 16 to 18-year-old in your first customer service role. Most people of that age group were shy, unsure of what to say, and lacking in confidence. Yet they were in a situation where they were expected to talk to strangers and sell them things.

In a lot of businesses, there is no induction program or structured sales training. Salespeople are thrown into serving customers at the sharp end and expected to not only survive, but to make sales and please customers.

Team players are told to approach customers and sell product. In many cases, team members lack the confidence, the technical product knowledge (*"You'll learn as you go"!*) and the communication skills. In addition, few salespeople understand the selling process. So, untrained salespeople gingerly go up to a customer and ask: *"Can I help you?"* The customer says *"no"*, and the salesperson often feels an inner sense of relief. He can then carry on filling or dusting shelves, as this is a task he can cope with within his comfort zone.

Alas, some salespeople are never given the opportunity to grow out of this scenario. I have had middle-aged salespeople attend workshops — people who have been in selling all their lives, but who have never understood their role in the community, until attending such a customer relationship workshop.

Building a Relationship in One Sentence

The key to success is to start building a relationship as soon as you start talking. There are a number of techniques you can use. Most depend on reading the customer to ensure you use the correct approach for the right situation. Let's look at the different approaches you can take when you start a conversation.

Firstly, you can divide the types of approach into four different styles:

- The social approach
- The merchandise approach
- The service approach
- The emotional approach

The Social Approach

The potential customer approaches you; you have no idea what they want, if anything at all. This eliminates the merchandise and service approaches.

The social approach is one in which you welcome and greet the customer with a complete sentence, one that has nothing to do with your product, service or services. It is a complete sentence that may be about the weather, sport, a recent event in both of your lives, or a reflective comment on what the customer has just experienced. Let me give you some examples to illustrate what I mean.

The weather
"Good morning, isn't it a lovely day today?"
"Good afternoon, wasn't it a bad storm last night? How did you cope?"

Sport
"Hi, did you see the game last night? Wasn't it a thriller!"
"G'day, who are you supporting tonight?"

A recent event in both your lives
A sad example of this was how the events in Washington, Pennsylvania and New York on September 11 2001 brought the whole of the Western world together.

On a more cheerful note, you may comment on a wedding or celebration you are aware of.

Reflective comment
I personally enjoy business people who use reflective comments, as it shows that they care about their client as a person. Reflective comments that have been used on me include:

"Good evening, how far have you driven today?" (When I am checking into a motel).
"Hi, how is the TV going you purchased from us?"
"Hi, how was your journey?"

The social approach is often under-used, yet it is a great way of building a relationship and opening up a conversation; let's use it more often.

The Merchandise Approach

If a potential customer is looking at a product, then you have an ideal opportunity to use the merchandise approach to make a sale.

The chances are that people pick a product up when they are in a buying mode. You can then use your background knowledge, and more importantly, your personal knowledge to start a conversation.

Openers such as:
"Hi, lovely oranges aren't they? I had one last night and they are really sweet."
"Hi, that wine goes great with fish. I had a glass last night with my meal."
"Good morning, that skirt has just come in from Italy. I just think it's gorgeous."
"That book is a really gripping novel, I couldn't put it down when I read it!"

Show that you have a personal involvement with the product and your customer is more inclined to believe you and build on the relationship.

Become A Power Spot Promoter As Well!

I have been expounding the value of 'power spots' for many years and airing the fact that they can increase your sales by around 540%. Yet I'm sure there are people who still doubt the impact of power displays. For those who are sceptical, consider the following situation as related to me by Ewan at "Paper Plus", Queenstown, in New Zealand.

Ewan purchased 480 toy kiwis (the national bird of New Zealand) to sell in his stationery shop and bookstore. After three months, he had sold 60 and his sales team was getting frustrated that the kiwis were taking up valuable sales space and losing money in the process.

In January, Ewan turned to the page in my book *'Just About Everything a Retail Manager Needs to Know'*, which discusses how to build power displays.

He followed the instructions and created a pyramid display of kiwis in a primary sales position. He made sure the signs indicated customer ownership, by using the word 'your' in the sign, and waited to see what would happen. In February he sold 198 kiwis and 143 in March — well above the projected 540% increase in sales.

Well done and many thanks to Ewan for his comments. I'd love to hear your success stories too!

A Position of Power – You Can Do It!

Here's a really essential technique we have adopted in our library consultancy services with Fiona Emberton, a consultant with the John Stanley team — the Power Display.

Our surveys have been telling us that library customers are unaware of even their most basic products and services. Yet librarians KNOW what goldmines libraries are, and that they can really *change lives*. Luckily, it doesn't take vast funding to improve customer perception and increase loans, just a little bit of know-how.

When you go to any well-run organisation, have a look as you enter — no good business would ever miss the opportunity to show off a new product or a special promotion (remember, a pyramid in the right spot can increase sales by 540%!).

Try this recipe in your library, or alter it to fit your store. Take a table and place in front of it a smaller one, about half the size, and a little tucked under. Then on top place a nest of saucepans, a string of onions, jar of wooden spoons, apron — and a smart sign placed at eye level on a stand. Add a combination of your best cookbooks, videos, and magazines — and watch your customers loving the ambience it creates!

You've probably been doing this for years, but the difference is the *position*. By placing it just about 5-10 metres inside — slap bang in front of customers — you've got a 'power position'. Fiona Emberton, when she was the Coordinator Community Liaison with Brisbane City Library Services, said they tried one in their busiest library, in a few places just metres apart, and once they found that magic power spot, the display had to be filled every 15 minutes or so. The result was happy, happy customers and less re-shelving!

The Service Approach

We've already discussed the fact that "Can I help you?" doesn't work, yet technically this is a service approach.

Service approaches can be split into three styles:
* A closed approach
* Open
* Leading

A Closed Approach

A closed approach results in a 'yes' or 'no' answer from the person you communicate with. Hence the 'closed' terminology, as this approach shuts down a conversation; it does not 'open up' verbal communication between two people. Therefore "Can I help you?" is a classic example of a closed approach.

There is a role for the closed approach in the game of selling. It can be used very effectively when answering the phone or when a puzzled customer walks directly up to you. Alas, the problem is that it is used far too much as an ineffective attempt to make a sale.

So, as a closed approach is now out of the question for most situations, what are the alternatives?

The Open Approach

I believe the *minimum* standard of approaching the customer should be the 'open' approach. People with young children are especially familiar with this technique. All open approaches start with:

How	Where
What	Why
When	Who

A question starting with any of the above words forces the respondent to construct a complete answer. You can then continue the conversation in whichever way is most suitable.

In retailing, "How can I help you?" is a great opener for people who fear using other ways of starting a conversation. Many businesses use this as their *minimum* standard in training, and I agree with their stance. It should be the minimum only.

Another question may be "What are you looking for?" DO ensure your team is trained to use open questions at least as effectively as their children use them!

Leading Your Customers Carefully

Leading service statements should be used with exceptional care. You may say something genuinely, but it could be perceived as 'pressure selling'. We all know how suspicious customers are of high-pressure sales people.

The leading approach to opening a conversation always ends with so-called 'it-isms'. For example:

"Lovely day, isn't it?"
"Good game yesterday, wasn't it?"
"It's worked especially well, hasn't it?"

Try this in the selling situation and you could get into deep trouble, however. For example:

"It is a lovely vehicle, isn't it?"
"Tastes wonderful, doesn't it?"

This is a great approach if the customer agrees with you. However, it's dangerous if he doesn't agree with you, but feels he should agree just to be polite.

The Emotional Approach – a Genuine Winner

Some people are born as natural salespeople. I know that many will argue that effective selling is a trainable function, and I am one of those people. I also have to accept that some people are born salespeople. Those people are the emotional sellers.

Generally, women are better emotional salespeople than men are. An emotional salesperson simply compliments the person they are talking to in the first sentence they use. It's that simple. Except that the majority of us, if we do it, sound insincere. An emotional salesperson sincerely compliments and the recipient knows it's a sincere comment.

He or she makes comments such as:

"Oh, you've got lovely hair!"

"I love the colour of your shirt."

"What a pretty dress!"

"That's a great tie!"

The above are all examples of emotional selling. But remember, this cannot be taught; it has to come from the heart. Emotional salespeople look for something they genuinely like in a person and compliment that person on it. If you can't find something you genuinely like about the person, don't try to use this technique — it won't work! Use a different approach.

I've often found that emotional salespeople can double the average sale per customer in comparison with non-emotional salespeople.

Get a team of emotional salespeople together and watch your business grow.

Today's Currency Is Knowledge

Your customer has access to more information today via their computer than they ever dreamt of in the past. The only benefit you can offer is a knowledge-added service that saves him the time of finding it himself.

But remember that in today's world, that customer has access to the same knowledge you have. Gone are the days when you could suggest that technical knowledge was exclusive to you.

Think FOR Your Customer

Three Key Actions

- Train all the team in the art of starting a conversation.
- Remember the team should be building relationships, not making sales.
- Monitor the team's verbal communications. It is a key to increasing the average sale.

My Action Plan

1. _____

_____

_____

_____

2. _____

_____

_____

3. _____

_____

_____

SECTION 5

How to Become an Effective Salesperson

– I Dare You to Close the Sale

How often have you seen a customer with a salesperson who has done an excellent job in selling the benefits of the product that the customer is interested in, but who then failed to close the sale?

The customer then often walks away feeling disappointed and wondering what went wrong. Why didn't the salesperson read the clues: was it that he was not watching for clues on when to close the sale, or was it that he lacked the confidence to do so?

Closing the sale is an art. There are numerous ways to close the sale and salespeople need to use a different technique for different situations. Each customer and situation is unique.

The worst dilemma for a salesperson is when the customer says "I'll think about it" or "I need to discuss it with my partner". Most salespeople know that these are signs that they have failed to close the sale and the consumer is trying to let them down lightly.

The point at which the salesperson should ask the buyer for his order is called the 'CLOSE'. Much of the effort in planned selling is wasted if the salesperson fails to effectively close the sale. It is evident that particular attention to the close is vital to the success of the sale.

- Tackle Closure with Confidence

No matter what technique is used to close a sale successfully, it is important that the process be undertaken positively, realistically, logically, confidently, and with appropriate timing. Always assume that you are going to get the order.

Use positive phrases. Never use questions such as "Would you like to have this?" or "Will this be enough?" Be persistent. Never give up at the first 'no' but be aware of the point when the order is totally lost and any further persistence will cause offence. Link your closing comments logically to the overall sales presentation.

Let your whole tone reflect your confidence in the proposition and show that you expect to sell the product. Keep your body language positive. Maintain eye contact with the customer.

- Select the Appropriate Close to Seal the Deal

Closure can usually be accomplished using one of a number of techniques. The type used will vary according to the situation and it should be the close (or closes) most suitable for that situation. Very often more than one close will be used. Consider, and apply as suitable, one or more of the following:

a) Summary Close

Sum up your sales story — particularly if you are interrupted by other customers, the telephone, or any other means. Then get down to quantities, in other words, "How many of those would you like?"

b) Physical Close

Some types of promotion make a very positive 'physical close' possible. You may, for example, be selling a bonus offer to the buyer and there is no more effective way of closing than actually giving him part of the bonus on the spot. "That is the bonus for you, just on this small order here."

c) Buyer's Remark

The buyer himself will often make some remark that will give you a lead into the close; eg "You were saying just now Mr Seller how well this line has sold recently..."

d) Minor Point

Very often the buyer has almost decided to buy, yet requires a minimum amount of persuasion to get final agreement on an order. A very effective method of closing in such circumstances is to check some point of detail with the buyer, such as, "Would you like a copy of the order?" or "Let me see, is it 21 or 23 High Street?"

e) Apparent Concession Close

Sometimes a part of an order may be too large, or contain unacceptable sizes or colours. This may or may not be deliberately planned. An acceptable way to close is to apparently give way on one part of the order "Obviously the 5-litre size is too much for you, so we can provide you with the 2.5-litre and 1-litre sizes if those suit you better."

f) Verbal Proof

This type of close is used when you quote the examples of other customers. "I have a customer on the other side of town and he felt this particular offer was ideal for his situation, which is very similar to yours."

g) Fear Close

The fear close emphasises the point that the customer will be missing something if he does not order now. You can stress that the deal is too good to miss or that if the customer does not take the product now then he may be losing out (appeal to the relevant buying motive). For example, one that is often used is "This is the last one in this colour/model/size..."

h) Isolation Close
    Very often you will attempt to close, yet find that the customer says 'no' to the order. You should try to isolate his reason for not buying. The customer has given an objection, so by utilising the formula of isolating the reason, and solving the objection, you can use it as an opportunity to close.

i) Alternative Close
    When using this type of close you get the customer's acceptance by asking which of two alternative orders he prefers. He may not then realise that a third alternative of not buying at all is open to him.

j) Assumptive Close
    Assume you are going to get the order and simply proceed to write it down. Care must be taken with this close to ensure timing is right. It is a very effective close when well executed.

Usually one of the preceding types of closes dominates but, more often than not, a combination of two types is successful in practice.

The important thing to remember about sealing a deal is 'never give up', as the following statistics reveal:

44% of sales people give up after one 'No'
22% of sales people give up after two 'No's'
14% of sales people give up after three 'No's'
12% of sales people give up after four 'No's'
In other words, 92% of sales people GIVE UP

Perhaps what they didn't know was that 60% of all customers say 'no' four times before saying YES.

Ref 'How to Win Customers and Keep Them for Life'
Michael Leboeuf, PhD, Berkley Books, New York (1989)
ISBN 0-425-11468-6.

Memo

Become Pro-active and Reduce Your Labour Costs by $30,000

McDonald's has a new CEO, Charles Bell. In his inaugural speech to the directors, he announced that if one more customer were serviced every two hours, each store would save $30,000 in wages per year.

How would one more sale an hour affect your business?

Think FOR Your Customer

Three Key Actions

- Train all the team members in the various skills used to close the sale.
- Remember NO doesn't necessarily mean NO.
- Train your team to look for the closure signs in your customers.

My Action Plan

1. _____

_____

_____

_____

2. _____

_____

_____

_____

3. _____

_____

_____

_____

Become a Matchmaker

Memo

Men and Christmas Don't Mix

It's that time of year again...

As you put your reindeer antlers on and prepare for the Christmas rush, spare a thought for that disadvantaged creature — the male shopper.

No, this isn't a joke. Its been scientifically proven! Well, a psychologist carrying out some research on behalf of an English shopping centre came up with some interesting findings.

You may remember hearing about it. Just prior to Christmas a couple of years ago, Brent Cross Shopping Centre in north London sent men and women of different ages to stores with identical Christmas lists. Some went alone, while others were accompanied by children.

Every man in the survey suffered a considerable increase in blood pressure and heart rate, while only one in four women registered a significant change.

For men, even the thought of going shopping was enough to send their stress levels soaring.

According to the study, over 70% of the men recorded above-average readings before even stepping out the front door. The challenge of choosing the right gift for loved ones and facing crowded shops and long queues was almost too much for them. In fact, according to the researcher, the peak stress levels were equivalent to emergency situations experienced by fighter pilots or policemen going into difficult situations.

This raises the question: "What can I do to eliminate or reduce my customer's stress in the busy lead-up to Christmas?" Here are some discussion points for you to consider. Talk these through with your team and come up with a series of recommendations that are right for your business.

continued next page...

The male shopper is likely to be less comfortable and confident about trends, sizes, colours, fragrances, and is often embarrassed about asking questions, particularly in 'female' shops. What can you do to make a male shopper feel more comfortable, to put him at ease and to start him talking about his shopping dilemma?

Blokes as a general rule are single-minded and they are likely to be focused on getting a present for one person, when they have two or three others to buy for. Wives and girlfriends get fed up buying the gifts for his parents or his children. So this is an opportunity for you to make him the hero. Find out whom else he should be buying for and suggest solutions. If you do, next year you will be his store of first choice for birthdays, Christmas, Valentine's and other special occasions. Help him with the box, the card, the gift-wrapping and all the little extras that will have him glowing with pleasure at how well he has done.

Who are the other 'disadvantaged' groups likely to be shopping in your organisation between now and Christmas (or any other special occasion)? Is it young children buying for a parent or a sibling? Is it the adult struggling with what to buy for teenage nieces and nephews? Is it the customer with language difficulties? Is it mum with her pusher, unable to get through crowded aisles or past special seasonal displays?

There is a lot to prepare for at this busy time of year. Make sure that catering for the special needs of your customers is the number one priority for all your team. Good luck and good trading!

Reference: Jurek Leon, Terrific Trading Pty Ltd, "Terrific Tips for Christmas"
e-mail: jurekleon@ozemail.com.au

Sell something — then sell something. The Americans often call this 'back-ending', but it's a golden rule of selling.

If a customer merely comes into an organisation and asks for a product or service and gives you his money, you've failed. A self-service operation would have been more profitable to the business.

Your role is to sell something after the customer has made his planned purchase, and no, I don't think this is pressure selling — I think it's professional selling.

You have a range of options in your selling approach, but we will discuss these later. Let me first tell you a true story that a delegate revealed in a workshop.

This particular person sold bedding plants in a garden centre; he was also a keen gardener himself. Each spring he purchased bedding plants from his own garden centre, plus slug and snail control pellets, as he lived in an area where if you didn't use a control such as this your plants would be eaten within a week.

When it came to selling plants to customers, our salesperson never mentioned slug and snail pellets. His view was that to offer an add-on product would be seen as pressure selling, and against his beliefs. When the rest of the group disagreed, he argued that everyone knows you need slug pellets and if people wanted them they would ask for them.

This salesman didn't understand his role as a solution provider or a 'matchmaker' and alas we didn't manage to change his views. He was adamant that whenever people buy they know exactly what they need. If only this was true. The majority of us don't have the time or skills to think through the project or problem — that's why we seek out sales experts to help us solve our problems.

The key is identifying how to be an effective matchmaker. That means you need to know your product, services, customers' needs, and how the customer is thinking (or not, as the case may be!) It's quite a challenge, and unfortunately, one that very few salespeople master.

Hence the term *'Think FOR Your Customer'* not *like* your customer. You need to anticipate his or her needs. Yes, you do need to put yourself in your customer's shoes, but you also need to be thinking for that customer. You have to become the customer's matchmaker and hero.

Think and Drink

In some buying situations the customer needs time on his own to think through the buying options. This could occur when buying kitchen units, furniture or garden features.

One of my clients provides its customers with 'Think and Drink' vouchers. A team member consulting with a client gives one of these vouchers to any customer they believe needs time on his own to look at all the options.

Does it work? It's far better to allow the customers to have private thinking time while they are with you rather than let them go home and think about it.

The Solutions Place

Hardware stores are traditionally known as places that attract males who want to obtain power tools, garden hoses and spanners. But, in a changing world, you need to target different groups to maximise your sales.

"Ace Hardware" in the USA is a good example of how a business has evolved from a place where you buy products into a place where your problems are solved.

One market with huge potential for hardware owners is the singles market. Is it a worthy target? Consider the facts from the USA Census Bureau:

	1970	2000
Median age of first marriage for women	21.4	25.1
Median age of first marriage for men	22.2	26.8
Elderly women over 65 living on own	-	19 million
Elderly men over 65 living on own	-	14 million
Single mothers	3 million	10 million

Ace Hardware traditionally sold to 35 to 54-year-old males with a family. John Venhuizsn, Ace's corporate marketing manager, is responsible for helping instigate a marketing shift. Keeping Ace's traditional target market, John decided to tackle the female and singles market by thinking for these potential customers.

Ace has subsequently created 'Solution Places' — a zone of softer colours and a friendlier environment where singles and women can relax with a member of the Ace team and discuss the queries they were afraid to ask in a more traditional 'male' environment.

How do you become a matchmaker? Firstly your team must become technical consultants. They must know their products.

I recently worked with a group of hardware stores that had 140 members in its group. The corporate motto was that they were the hardware 'experts'. The leading store in the group had an average sale that was twice that of the second most successful store in the chain.

When I talked to members, they believed they were the experts in hardware. When I asked how often they conducted product knowledge training sessions, they gave me blank looks. For the majority, it was 'never'. They then told me that team members learn on the job and asked if I knew how difficult it was to organise regular training meetings?

Later on I worked in-house with the leading retailer in the group, whose representative had kept quiet during the earlier discussions.

He mentioned that a 30-minute product knowledge session on Wednesday mornings was compulsory for all team members. He and his team believed they were the best because they were the best technically. It definitely showed up in the average sale per customer.

Matchmaking starts with team members having confidence in their technical skills and product knowledge. Don't leave this to chance and previous experience. Product knowledge sessions should be in integral part of your culture.

The second key to matchmaking is having the ability to build matchmaking displays. Create the bedroom, patio, kitchen, dining experience or fashion statement — don't sell individual products.

Provide consumer 'reminder' signs. The following work brilliantly:

Don't forget -
you may need:

- Quality planting mix ☐
- Plant food ☐
- Plant care items ☐
- Tree stakes ☐
- Plant ties ☐
- Patio tubs ☐
- A gift for a loved one ☐

Ask our friendly team if you would like further advice, we're delighted to help you.

DON'T FORGET

The more skilled your team members are at matchmaking, the more likely you are to increase the average sale per customer.

Think FOR Your Customer

Three Key Action Points

- Ensure you have 'matchmaker' displays in your business that customers understand and can relate to.
- Ensure you have relevant 'reminder' signs in your business for add-on sales.
- Have compulsory product knowledge training sessions for the team.

My Action Plan

1. _____

_____

_____

_____

_____

2. _____

_____

_____

_____

3. _____

_____

_____

_____

Think FOR Your Customers

Over the years, various authors have written books on customer service. The theme of these books has basically revolved around thinking *like* a customer. But, times change and customers and businesses change with them.

Potential customers today have less time than ever before, and in addition they are now getting an information overload. If in today's market you thought like a customer, the chances are you'd be as stressed and confused as many of them are!

In the first chapter, I mentioned David Lewis and Darren Bridge's recent book *'The Soul of the New Consumer: Authenticity, What We Buy and Why in the New Economy'*. They conducted research into what stressed consumers when they went shopping. To recap, their research identified the major contributors to stress as:

1. Congestion in aisles
2. Delays at queues
3. Difficulty in locating products
4. Loud music
5. Too hot/cold
6. Lighting too bright/dim
7. Public announcements
8. Confusing store layout
9. Inefficient and bad signage
10. Bad labelling

In modern trading, if you wish to grow your market share, then it is essential to think FOR customers, rather than think like them. For some businesses this means training their teams to think in a completely new way.

Let me give you another example. I recently carried out some work for a Dutch retailer. He had analysed his market and found that his consumers ate grapefruit at breakfast. His team agreed to move the grapefruit to the breakfast aisle and place them next to the breakfast cereals. The result was grapefruit sales increased considerably, due to the retailer thinking FOR his customers, and thereby making life easier for them.

I mentioned this idea to a team in an Australian supermarket. They agreed that Australian consumers also eat grapefruit at breakfast. However, this team stated that the correct location for grapefruit was in the fruit department, next to the oranges. I failed in my attempt to get the store to test the concept. Why? The team was not prepared to think FOR its customers. The result was no increase in grapefruit sales.

In today's hectic world, customers don't have time to think through all of the intricate details of their daily needs and wants. Today's customers need you to do their thinking for them, they need you to take care of the business of their daily needs. This means a number of strategies need to be considered, such as:

1. Getting away from your old 'category' thinking when you are merchandising. Think about category merchandising based on how customers live their lives, and think through their needs. Then you need to manage your categories in a way that helps customers make their necessary purchases.

   I recently worked with a group of garden centres where the trees were the responsibility of the plant manager and placed in one section of the centre. The tree stakes were the responsibility of the 'wood products' category manager and were at the opposite end of the retail area. The category managers were happy. However, customers often left the centre having purchased a tree without a tree stake, or else they were confused about where to find a stake, due to the category management. The result was lost sales and disappointed customers who went home to plant their tree, and then realised they had forgotten to purchase a stake.

2. A paint trader client of mine had a different approach to helping his customers think through the details of the job ahead of them. When a customer purchased paint, he provided a checklist of items needed to complete the job successfully. This was a simple but effective way of thinking for the customer. All the customer had to do was tick the checklist. This type of checklist could be used in many situations to help customers through the decision-making process of their projects. The key is to put the checklist on a 'jotter pad' that your team members can keep in their top pockets. If you do this it's more likely to be used, rather than if it's a handout at the counter — where it is often too late in the shopping experience to be of benefit for the customer.

3. Team training on how customers think and what information they need is critical. Too often sales teams take for granted that customers know more than they do. Plus, the team needs to realise that women buy and think differently to men. In his book 'Why We Buy, The Science of Shopping' (Touchstone Books; June 2000, ISBN: 0684849143), Paco Underhill identifies this exceptionally well. His research found that women will generally purchase a portable phone based on one visit to the store. Men, on average, took three visits before they made their purchase. This was because sales assistants didn't understand how men purchased portable phones. The signage in phone stores is often confusing. Women will ask the sales assistant to explain the jargon, whereas many men are too embarrassed to ask for an explanation. They will leave the store and do their own research rather than appear ignorant, returning later to the store to make their purchase. Skills training for the team would have resulted in saving time for their customers and increased sales for the business, creating a 'win:win' situation.

4. As customers, we are often placed in situations where we don't understand the product and need 'comfort' or 'reassurance' statements on signage in the business. Airport bookstores tend to do this exceptionally well by introducing 'Best Seller' categories through their signage. They know that many people only read a book when they fly and thus their knowledge of what to read may be limited. The consumer is reassured by 'Best Seller' signage. He or she believes a best seller must be a good read and that a book from this category will not disappoint.

The same promotional strategy works well in music stores and in liquor stores. However, many businesses miss the opportunity to introduce it to their clients. This type of reassurance would work well anywhere that clients may lack confidence in their buying decision, especially in outlets like garden centres, hardware stores, delicatessens and health shops. Outside of ladies fashion stores, it is guaranteed to work!

The key is to think FOR your customers, because as they get busier, they need you to do more thinking for them!

Think FOR Your Customer

Three Key Action Points

- Produce checklists based on tasks, that your team can use with customers.
- Keep signage simple so that your customer can easily understand it.
- Don't let category managers control the thinking process based on product type. Merchandise how a customer would think.

My Action Plan

1. _____

   _____

   _____

   _____

2. _____

   _____

   _____

   _____

3. _____

   _____

   _____

   _____

SECTION 6

Everyone Is Different

Traditionalists will tell you that everyone should be treated the same way. I cannot accept that. I believe that everyone is an individual and should be treated accordingly.

We demand different levels of customer service, depending on our age, gender, loyalty, and other variables. Yes, there should be a minimum level of consistency in your customer service, but apart from that you should vary your service based upon your individual customer's needs and wants.

Service Variance Depending On Age

Memo

Debbie Allen's Top 10 Success Strategies that she lists on her webpage are:

1. Believe in yourself
2. Have revolutionary thoughts
3. Visualise your success
4. Never stop learning and growing
5. Have a positive attitude
6. Be open-minded and flexible
7. Be professional and honest
8. Service with diversity (by this Debbie is referring to being aware of the different needs of your customers)
9. Network strategically
10. Brand your uniqueness

Ref: www.DebbieAllen.com

Our expectations change as we get older and therefore your customer service policy needs to reflect these life changes.

Let's take a journey through the ages to find examples of how this could change.

Toddlers

Toddlers are potential customers; they can influence where their parents shop. Ensure that your team acknowledges this group — otherwise they may be influencing their parents to shop elsewhere. My own daughter, as a toddler, always wanted us to visit our local garden centre. Why? The team members there always went out of their way to say "hello" to her and offer her something. This was often a flower that had dropped from a plant. Those team members made her feel that she was special to them. She always took those flowers home and treasured them.

You may want to give toddlers a candy, balloon or other small present. It works, but get their parents' permission first. Remember, just saying hello and warmly recognising their presence can be enough to start them asking their parents to make a return visit. How many toddlers have learnt "McDonald's" as one of his or her first words? McDonald's is a company that recognises the power of toddlers. In the USA, Ronald McDonald is better known than Father Christmas, which proves its target marketing was effective.

Children – Remember PESTER Power

Many businesses have developed children's clubs, whether it is a cooking club, gardening club or a sewing club. Ideally, these clubs are designed to fit into school holidays. They can enhance sales by promoting projects that use products that are available in the store. One of the keys to success is to ensure that the person coordinating such a club can relate to this audience, ie you need somebody who enjoys working with children and can easily relate to them.

Teenagers

Many businesses find this a difficult age group to relate to. Whilst children are sociable with all groups, teenagers tend to want their own space and can often only relate within their own social group.

Some organisations have environments that attract this group. If this is a market group that you want to attract, then perhaps get a group of teenagers together into an informal focus group and discuss with them how they like a store to be laid out. Then think carefully about how they relate to each other and what their priorities are when you are planning your strategy. Remember, if baby-boomers find the environment you've created to be comfortable, you've got it wrong for teenagers! The ambience that will attract teenagers is at the other end of the scale to that which attracts baby-boomers.

Some libraries cater for this group exceptionally well. Libraries are known as quiet places where you can obtain information, mostly from books.

However, some of my library clients have 'youth zones', complete with Coca-Cola machines, computer access and leisure furniture. To make them work, they invited youth to design and decorate them. The traditional libraries may be horrified, but today's youth are now enjoying an environment they would not have considered using in the past.

Generation X

'Generation X' is very 'computer savvy'. Its members are generally hi-tech users, but are often unaware of product detail. Whatever you do, don't embarrass members of this group.

Memo

Understanding Generation X

This generation is well educated, driven, and confident of their abilities. They grew up reading 'Just Do It' billboards and believing them, as they have never experienced a recession.

This generation wants it now, as can be seen from their acceptance of fast food, on-line shopping and Internet banking.

If you employ Generation X-ers and you want to keep them, you need to provide performance-related incentives, create a work environment they like, and ask them what they want. If you get it right, they may decide YOU deserve some loyalty.

Ref: Unknown.

Generation X is an important group of consumers. In Australia it makes up 26% of the population, compared to the 25% of the population that is the baby-boomers. Generation X tends to have a tight social group of friends, and its members look for pragmatic answers to their problems — they are not dreamers.

Generation X is the most sceptical group when it comes to marketing. Its members don't believe in absolute truths and are looking for immediate gratification.

In retail terms, this is the 'Do It Yourself' (DIY) market. The category killers (businesses who dominate a specific product range and provide a wide and deep range of product in the section) and box stores (large retail sheds) of the world have developed their businesses by targeting this group. The box stores know that members of this sector have home improvement desires and are prepared to buy the different elements to create the environment they want, and they will do it themselves.

Baby-Boomers

This group has led the business revival over the last few decades and since their 'hippy' days, by sheer volume of numbers, has demanded to continue to lead the way. It has now evolved into the 'Do It for Me' (DIM) market. Its members don't have time to do it themselves, but they do have money. As a result, this segment will pay for service, to have it done for them.

Over the last few years we've seen huge growth in the service industry aimed at this market sector. Housekeeping, garden services, "Hire-a-Hubby", and other home service franchises have grown rapidly. Plus, when members of this sector of the market go shopping, they often want it now, wrapped and delivered, accompanied by exceptional customer service. Plus, it must be convenient, as they don't have time to shop.

Baby-boomers are the most demanding people in society. But they are prepared to pay for the services provided. Just make sure your team members are prepared for their demands. They have changed how meat retailers do business. Wait for the changes in the funeral industry!

The 'Grey Tigers'

We are all now living longer on average than ever before in the history of mankind. In Australia there are now 2.3 million

---

Memo

Arabic Coca-Cola

A disappointed Coca-Cola salesman returns from his Middle East assignment. A friend asks, "Why weren't you successful with the Arabs?"

The salesman explains, "When I got posted to the Middle East, I was very confident that I would makes a good sales pitch, as Cola is virtually unknown there. But, I had a problem — I didn't know how to speak Arabic. So, I planned to convey the message through 3 posters...

First poster: a man crawling through the hot desert sands... totally exhausted and panting.

Second: the man is drinking our Cola, and...

Third: our man is now totally refreshed.

Then these posters were pasted all over the place."

"That should have worked," says the friend.

The salesman replies, "Well, not only did I not speak Arabic, I also didn't realize that Arabs read from right to left..."

Source: Unknown

people over 65 years old. This sector, the 'grey tigers', is going to increase rapidly over the next decade.

Businesses need to remove the stress of shopping for this age group, if they are to obtain its members' loyalty. Can the elderly easily walk around your premises? Are products located so older people can easily pick them up? Can older persons easily handle the products you are selling? Are you aware of the needs of this sector? For example, can you imagine opening a petrol cap if you have arthritis?

As the size of this market sector increases, the services offered by retailers and service providers like tradespeople will have to change to meet its needs. Businesses that identify the needs of this group, and create a strategy to fill those needs, will have a successful few decades ahead of them.

Service Variance Depending On Gender

It's not only an age factor; the service provided to customers has a gender factor too. Women and men shop differently. Basically, women generally are the 'social shoppers' and men generally are the 'destination shoppers'. Men select what they want to buy, go to the shop, purchase it, and return with the minimum of browse shopping.

But men, shopping on their own when relaxed, will often spend more money, as they are in general less price-sensitive than women are. The role of the business manager is to relax male shoppers in order to encourage this market sector to spend more time and money in the premises.

Memo

Thinking FOR the Customer May Mean Separating the Sexes!

The Hilton in London has opened up a women-only floor in its hotel. This is based on the needs of female travellers who want safe, female-friendly environments.

Women check in at a private area and food is delivered via room service by female staff. The floor is monitored 24-hours-a-day by security cameras.

The result is believed to be a net gain of 5% more women using the hotel.

This result is based on research that showed:

- 42% of women travellers worry about security
- 29% found themselves in threatening situations
- 78% choose hotels based on safety grounds

Ref: The Sunday Times, South Africa, April 6 2003

Memo

"Hunters" and "gatherers" at your local mall

Men and women shop differently — and it could be due to our primeval instincts.

A new study sponsored by the British credit card company Barclaycard surveyed 60 male and female shoppers about their habits in the mall.

It found that seven in ten men were likely to fit the traditional "hunter" profile — they knew exactly what they wanted, and preferred to "go in for the kill" once they found what they were looking for.

Eight in ten women fitted the "gatherer" model — they liked to browse and consider their options before making a purchase. This made them "better" shoppers — they were more likely to get a good deal because of their more deliberate approach.

The survey also looked at how long it took for men and women to get tired of shopping. On average, men tended to wear out after 72 minutes of browsing, while the women could keep going for a further 28 minutes before they'd had enough.

Ref: http://www.exn.ca/Stories/2003/09/18/51.asp

Let me give you one example.

I was recently shopping with my wife in Wellington, New Zealand. We passed, or nearly passed, an up-market ladies fashion shop and Linda commented on the ladies' blouses. I was instantly directed into the shop. At the far end of the shop was a settee, and since I realised we would be in the shop for some considerable time, I headed for the settee and sat down ready for a long stay. The sales assistant came up and asked if I was OK. I got a very strange look when I mentioned I was, but would like a coffee and newspaper. The result was that, after selecting one blouse, Linda read my embarrassed body language and came to the rescue. We purchased one blouse instead of the two or three she would have liked to try on — and very likely purchase.

The message is, if you don't make the men feel relaxed and welcome, then your average sale will be a lot less than it could otherwise be. If you want to increase your customer count, then encourage men to feel comfortable and to linger longer.

Consider the following:
* Offer current newspapers and sports magazines. (Can someone explain to me why doctors' surgeries rarely have today's newspaper in the waiting room and often only contain twelve-month-old women's magazines?)

- Provide complimentary coffee and water, where it's appropriate, to encourage males to relax.
- Separate male and female browse product areas, as a couple separated will spend more money.
- Use male colours in predominantly male shopping zones; eg power tools in hardware. Make men feel comfortable in these areas rather than women (unless you are targeting the female market — see earlier this chapter).

Memo

Don't Think Like a Caucasian

We live in a multicultural world and need to think FOR all cultures.

Think about Hispanic consumers in the USA, who comprise the largest minority group.

30% prefer to shop as a family.
25% of children are significantly influenced by brand.

Compared to Caucasians, Hispanics are twice as likely to search out a new store.

When it comes to fashion:

36% of Hispanics like to wear the latest fashions.
46% of Caucasians like to wear the latest fashions.
58% of blacks like to wear the latest fashions.

In San Ysidro, California, "Albertson's", a supermarket company, has opened a Hispanic store — now that's thinking FOR your customer.

Ref: Mediamark Research, USA, 2003.

One of my favourite retail establishments "Klownz", was a hairdresser in New Zealand. This company was excellent at looking at the needs and comforts of its customers. The entrance to the hairdressing salon was via a reception area that was complete with complimentary coffee, a sofa, and a piano. Children were directed into a child-friendly room where they could sit on an elephant or lion-shaped chair to have their hair cut, while they watch Disney videos.

Women were directed to a soft-coloured room, complete with fresh flowers, and men to a room where the colour scheme was almost black. A TV sat in the corner of the male area, showing global sports and the men may have been offered a beer. The company carefully read its customers and provided a leisurely environment for each targeted group.

Take a close look at who your real customers, clients, patients or visitors are. Are you clearly targeting them, or do you need to re-examine your strategy?

Not everyone is the same — treat people differently.

Think FOR Your Customer

Three Key Action Points

- Remember — we are all individuals, with individual expectations when it comes to service.
- Men shop and think differently to women. Ensure the team understands the differences.
- Relax the men, and women will buy more.

My Action Plan

1. _____

   _____

   _____

   _____

   _____

2. _____

   _____

   _____

   _____

3. _____

   _____

   _____

   _____

   _____

Provide What the Customer Expects and You Will Fail

How many businesses do you rave about to friends? Think about it; you and I visit numerous businesses every day. The majority do their job and provide satisfactory customer service. There is nothing wrong with that. But if you want to grow your business, you can't provide mere satisfaction. Satisfaction won't grow your business. What you need is what Stephen Blanchard and Robert Lorber, authors of '*One Minute Manager*' (Willow Books, London, ISBN 0-00-218118-5) would call a 'Raving Fan Policy'.

Memo

In a talk given in 2002 by Glenn Capelli (an Australian consultant from The True Learning Centre in Perth, Western Australia) stated that he believed businesses should do the following:

Eliminate customer sacrifice.

Increase customer satisfaction.

Create customer surprise.

Customers have to rave about you, and not take you for granted. OK, so you want your customers to become raving fans — how do you do that?

Firstly, where do you sit in your customer's mind? How good are you, compared to your competitors?

The first challenge is to shop at your competition and to check how they compare with your offer. Your competition is other businesses that are chasing for a share of your customer's wallet. They may not be providing the same product but they are still competing for the same dollars in your customer's wallet.

Every business has:

1. Competitors Those fighting for wallet share, but that don't sell identical items to you.

   For example, restaurants have competitors in the theatre, cinemas and other leisure activity industries.

2. Competition Those fighting for wallet share, but that do sell identical items to you.

   The above restaurant's competition is other restaurants within its designated catchment area.

Encourage your team members to visit competitors and competition and to report back to the rest of the team on their experiences. If you don't check out your competitors and your competition, you may be developing a false sense of security.

Have a 'Chow Now' Policy

The term 'chow now' comes from "Chef Allen's" restaurant in North Miami Beach, Florida, USA. On a regular basis, the owner gives $50 to each chef to spend on a meal at a similar restaurant to her own. You can imagine the comments that come back: "The plates are cold", "The sauce is too sweet", and so on. Obviously, the intention is to make sure Chef Allen's doesn't make the same mistakes.

A few years ago I was working with a client in New Zealand. The team members were confident they didn't need more customer service training. Prior to the meeting, we gave them $40 to spend in their local community. When they came back, they ran the meeting. On a whiteboard, we listed the weaknesses and strengths of the businesses they had visited. Alas, the board was full of weaknesses and hardly any strengths! It suddenly dawned on the team that, in their customers' eyes, they would be perceived in exactly the same way. From that point onward we could construct a meaningful customer service workshop based on an agenda that the team members set.

Don't be afraid to have a 'chow now' policy in your business; it will keep the team focused on the true objectives.

Delight Your Customers

I first came across the magic formula, 'Delight = Expectations +1', when listening to a presentation in the UK by Chris Daffey, the British customer service guru.

This formula is so simple and easy to implement that we often forget it. Think about it. Provide what the customer expects, as your average provider of customer service, and the result is that your customer does not talk about you. However, if you provide one extra benefit that customer does not expect, and your customer is delighted, he or she will talk about you to friends and family.

Since learning about this concept, I have come across a number of examples, both good and bad, that indicate how important it is.

In Australia, a client of mine was to be visited for the first time by the president of the company, who was based in South Africa. The company did its homework beforehand and found out that the president had a passion for yellow roses, Belgian chocolates, Italian food and Shiraz wine. All of these 'plus ones' were provided on this first visit. The president was impressed and mentioned he'd be back on a regular basis. I queried how the client was going to delight the leader next time, and was rewarded with puzzled faces.

Don't provide more than one 'plus one' at a time, as creating delight is an ongoing process. The 'plus one' has to create excitement. Provide the unexpected and charm the customer. To do that, you have to anticipate customers' needs. That's the real key to delighting customers.

Chris Daffey provides an example based on a travel agent in the United Kingdom. The travel agent sells holidays in Turkey to his UK clients. Most travel agents sell the holiday, mail the air tickets to the holiday-makers, and send them on their way with a cheery letter hoping that they enjoy their vacation.

Memo

Create an Experience for Your Customers

The "Five Flies" restaurant in Amsterdam, Holland has customised each dining chair based on personalities who have sat there. Each chair has a plaque on it telling customers the most famous person who has sat in it.

You could sit in the same chair as a Prime Minister, movie or sports star. It gets people talking.

Once the travellers arrive at the Turkish airport, they collect their luggage from the carousel, realise they cannot use the luggage trolleys (as they need a Turkish lira coin to hire the trolley), and find that the currency exchange offices are located on the other side of customs. The tourists then struggle with their luggage through Turkish customs control.

Our 'hero' travel agent sends his clients their airline tickets with a letter as well. However, taped to his 'have a nice holiday' letter is a Turkish lira coin for the luggage trolley dispenser. In his letter, he explains to his clients what the coin is for. His clients pull out their letter, retrieve the coin, and smugly insert it into the trolley dispenser machine. Imagine how they feel, when other tourists come up to them and ask where they got the coin from, and they reply, "My travel agent gave it to me!"

You don't need to invest a lot of money to become your clients' hero!

In Australia, there is a car service dealership that leaves a bunch of flowers, movie tickets or chocolates on the passenger seat of the vehicles it services. At every service the dealer leaves a different gift for his clients, who can't wait to get their car serviced with him to find out what their gift is this time!

I know a landscape designer who provides his customers with a bunch of flowers when he has completed the job. It is his way of saying 'thank you for the opportunity to work for you'.

I also know of a hardware store that provides a complimentary barbecue pack of meat when a customer buys a barbecue.

In Christchurch, New Zealand is the "Not Just Bears" teddy bear shop. It is a sole store, but understands how to delight the customer. I came across it when conducting a customer service workshop. After the session the owners invited me and the conference organiser to their store. We discovered a unique store selling hundreds of different types of teddy bears.

However, it was only when you purchased a teddy bear that you came across the true delight. My colleague purchased a $20 bear. When she paid, she was provided with a complimentary 'birth certificate' for the bear and asked if she needed a 'passport' for her bear. The passport cost $2.50 and was a miniature version of a normal passport. It was quickly snapped up and all the bear's details were written in it.

The bear travelled around the country and had his passport stamped at every airport. It kept dozens of people delighted and was an excellent promotional campaign for the store, plus she paid extra to be delighted. What can you do in your business?

I recently flew around the world with the "One World" airline group. I'm a platinum cardholder with one of the airlines in the group. On one of my recent flights the steward gave me a bottle of champagne and thanked me for my loyalty to the airline. I was impressed!

Delighting a customer is about providing the 'plus one', which must be of high value to the customer and low cost to you.

Brainstorm the opportunities in your business. I'm confident that the list can become quite long.

The key to success is to remember that, to delight the customer, you have to keep changing the 'plus one'. Once your customer comes to expect a particular 'plus one' then it has lost its ability to delight and has become an expectation. Remember — expectation plus one equals delight. The bad news is that customers' expectations are increasing and customers are also becoming more critical. But I believe you have no choice — it's delight or fail.

The challenge is:

- Excite your customers and create the RAVE factor in your business. Get your team to brainstorm 'WOW' ideas. If team members think them up, they are more likely to implement them.

- Don't provide boring or satisfactory service. Even invoices can have inspiring quotes on them to entertain your customers.

- Dare to be Different. You must make your business stand out from the rest. What can you do to differentiate your services, or service and product mixes?

- Think FOR your customer, not like them.

- Remember you will make mistakes, they are inevitable, but dissatisfied customers are not.

Think FOR Your Customer

Three Key Action Points

- Remember — you have competitors and competition. Make sure you 'mystery shop' at both, so you understand who is fighting for your wallet share and know their strengths and weaknesses.
- Develop a 'delight policy' for your business.
- Only exceed customer expectation by a factor of one.

My Action Plan

1. _____

_____

_____

_____

2. _____

_____

_____

3. _____

_____

_____

_____

SECTION 7

Building Ongoing Relationships

Being in business is about developing lifetime relationships with your customers. To achieve this, you need to develop a trusting relationship with them. Remember — people trust people, rather than businesses.

Building trust is easier in some businesses than in others. "The MJB&B Group", an Australian marketing group, produced some interesting findings in its January 2001 'The Battle Lines Are Drawn' report. It analysed trust factors in various businesses.

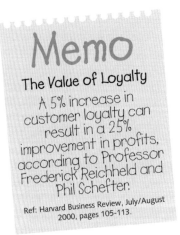

Memo

The Value of Loyalty

A 5% increase in customer loyalty can result in a 25% improvement in profits, according to Professor Frederick Reichheld and Phil Schefter.

Ref: Harvard Business Review, July/August 2000, pages 105-113.

Company type	Level of trust
	10 = complete trust 1 = no trust
Major charities	8.06
National TV	7.11
Wine companies	6.56
Airlines	6.37
Food manufacturers	5.89
Large retailers	5.82
Utility companies	5.71
Breweries	5.45
Motor vehicle companies	5.25
Sporting bodies	5.20
Telecommunications companies	4.89
Mining companies	4.52
Government departments	4.43
Insurance companies	4.13
Oil companies	4.02
Advertising agencies	3.80
Banks	3.47

Perception is the name of the game. As the above table illustrates, some businesses have to work harder than others to build an ongoing relationship.

Do Consumers Trust Retailers?

Well, according to work by Chris Ohlinger, CEO of "Service Industry Research Systems" (SIRS) in the USA, retailers have a long way to go.

Chris carried out work on trust factors with consumers in 2001 and it makes interesting reading, offering retailers some real challenges.

Firstly, he analysed satisfaction ratings of customers when they went to retail establishments.

The results are as follows:

Store Conditions	52% satisfaction rating
Selection of Products	49% satisfaction rating
Quality of Product	47% satisfaction rating
Service Provided	44% satisfaction rating
Price of Product Sold	41% satisfaction rating
Trust the Retailer	35% satisfaction rating

It is because of these figures that Chris believes that if retailers could improve trust levels, a 25% increase in bottom line could be achieved with the same customers.

Since 11 September 2001, consumers have become more concerned about safety and the welfare of their families. They have a low level of trust in many businesses and have started to search out businesses they feel they can trust.

This is reflected in another piece of work that Chris Ohlinger carried out.

He analysed performance versus potential of various retailers and analysed what wallet share each retailer got out of the potential market within the category in the catchment area. His figures highlight the importance of trust to the bottom line.

The weakest retailer in the catchment area obtained 15% of wallet share; this compared with 24% for the average retailer, 37% for the best and 46% for the best retailer in the category in the catchment area.

The key is to increase consumer trust, but how does an organisation go about it?

It's back to thinking FOR the customer and putting yourself in the customer's shoes.

Consumers trust businesses that:

- Think of THEIR welfare
- Think what's best for THEIR family
- Save THEM time

- Save THEM money
- Relate products to THEIR needs, based on the customer's own experiences

This does not mean an organisation must provide the cheapest product or service. If, for example, you were a retailer of tyres seeking to build trust in the market, you would emphasise the following:

- The need for customers to protect their families by having their tyres checked.
- Provide a tyre-checking service at the convenience of the customer.
- Emphasise that possibly a more expensive tyre will save money, as it will last longer.
- Discuss your customer's style and type of driving and provide a tyre suitable to his needs.

Remember that it is the most trusted organisation in each category that grows its market share.

The sales team and the marketing team must work together to ensure the promotion works. To develop a permission-marketing promotion campaign, you will need a system, and a reason, to collect existing customers' names and addresses. Customers will not volunteer this information without the reward of a benefit to them.

The reason could be to send out a newsletter to customers that will interest them or increase their knowledge of the products or services that you offer. It could be a 'loyalty card' that rewards their loyalty to your business, or it could be the formation of a club. Your customers will need to see an added value or some sort of enhanced status for themselves, before they will be encouraged to join in the program. You will need a standard form for them to complete, which should include a request for customer's name, address, telephone, e-mail, interests, birthday and other relevant information.

Once you have obtained this information, then you need a database that will enable you to record and retrieve information quickly and easily. There are a number of excellent database software programs on the market. Talk to your local experts, tell them what you want to achieve from using a database, and ask them to suggest a suitable product to meet your needs. Then talk to other people who have used the same database and get their views on its effectiveness, its strengths and weaknesses.

Once you have a database set up you can look at building relationships with your customers.

Don't bombard your customers with information. If you bombard them they will feel that this is not a caring relationship you are building, but a sales campaign. Relationship building takes time. Researchers have found that if you care about customers, you will communicate with them approximately every 90 days, or once a season. Remember that the word is 'communicate' — this is not a high-power selling tool.

There are various ways to communicate. Below is just a short review of some of the more common means of permission marketing. Brainstorm ideas with your team on ways to communicate with your customer base — the list can be endless.

Postcards

Postcards are a valuable way of showing people you care. Two effective ways I recommend are firstly to send a postcard to introduce a new season. For example, spring is coming; or autumn fashions have just arrived.

Make sure these cards have a picture of a person on them, and that they are the types of card the receiver may like to keep. People relate more easily to images of people on marketing campaigns. It adds a human touch and helps customers to relate in a meaningful way. We are all in the people industry, whatever we sell.

Secondly, next time you go on holiday, take the names and addresses of your top targeted customers and send them all a postcard from your destination. The more remote and exotic the destination the better.

When you get there, put stamps on the card and a note. "I'm on holiday, but I've seen a great idea to help your business, garden, project, etc — I'll call you on my return." Mail them off straight away but remember to follow through when you get home.

Inspirational Cards

In our own business we select certain clients and after finishing a contract send them a business motivational card. This normally goes out about two weeks after the event. It is amazing how many offices I go into six months later and the card is still in pride of place in the office.

Send Birthday Cards, Don't Send Christmas Cards

I can hear you say, "We always send Christmas cards!" You can send Christmas cards if you choose to, but don't classify them as a relationship-building tool. The Christmas card will get lost amongst all the others. Your business won't stand out from the crowd.

Send cards of celebration that make your business stand out from the crowd.

Send birthday cards, or...
Groundhog Day cards
St Patrick's Day cards
Australia Day cards
St George's Day cards...

You get the idea. Pick those events that other people have passed by and that way your business will stand out from the crowd.

Memo

What would you do if you walked into a hotel and saw this sign?

"Dear guests — we need your help. The mother of one of our housekeepers passed away and the funeral is this afternoon. Since our housekeeper is very shaken we all felt that we should be at the funeral. As such, there will be only one employee on site this afternoon. We appreciate your understanding, thanks!"

Well, it did occur at a Miami hotel recently. The hotel customers immediately shifted into a helping mode and served each other coffee in the lobby. Customers greeted new guests and explained the situation. Everyone was patient, tolerant and even enjoyed the experience.

This incident shows what can happen when you exceed customers' expectations. When you have a problem, customers get involved and love the novelty of the experience.

Ref: Chip R Bell, "Attracting and Keeping Customers for Life" Executive Excellence Publishing..

The Delia Effect – Personality Marketing

Clients purchase more products from business people who have personality and confidence. Organisations should recruit for personality; a team member's confidence then grows as knowledge increases.

In some industries, such as hardware, gardening, health and

food, we find that the media (and especially the TV) have a huge effect on the market. If you're in one of these industries, the consumers expect you to have at least the same knowledge as they do. Customers are often getting their knowledge from weekly 'lifestyle programs'. In the UK this is now known as the 'Delia Effect'. The saying comes from the huge following of English TV presenter Delia Smith's cooking programs, but also applies to the "Naked Chef " and "Nigella Bites" cooking programs, and gardening and home improvement programs.

According to major businesses in the UK, if a TV guru mentions a product or service, businesses can expect sales of that product or service to increase by 20% during the next seven trading days.

This means that the 'best of the best' businesses have to be in tune with what is being presented on TV and each team member has to be aware of what is being presented to their consumers if they are to build on the sale.

Different businesses have different approaches, but don't ignore the impact the Delia Effect can have on your business.

- Share TV programs between your team so each team member watches one TV program a week and reports back to the team on the key issues that will affect your business ON THE MORNING FOLLOWING the TV program.
- Create 'As Seen on TV' signs and place them next to relevant topical products.
- Have a white board in the staff room and use it to indicate what products were mentioned on TV during the week.
- If you don't stock the product that has been mentioned by the presenter, make sure all the team can offer a suitable substitute.
- Group together products that were mentioned on the TV program. If the presenter has written a book, put that book next to the product display.
- Obtain dummy televisions that you can use as a permanent display and arrange products around it that were mentioned during the week on the TV.
- Never say to a customer that you don't watch the TV show and don't ever criticise the presenter. These presenters are your customers' heroes and you should respect that when you are talking to your customers.

- Being 'on the ball' with what is on TV also indicates you are 'on the ball' as a business; it's a sure way of growing your business.

Newsletters — the '7 minute read'

Newsletters are now a common promotional tool and in some cases have been overdone. They have developed in three distinctive ways. Companies such as "Sainsbury's" supermarkets in the UK now produce a full magazine which consumers pay for. These newsletters can now be up to 100 pages in length and are literally glossy magazines. Within the magazine are vouchers for targeted products. The voucher value exceeds the price of the magazine, to make the readers feel they are getting value for money.

Memo

The Power of TV

According to David Domeney in the UK, the 'encouragement to buy' indicator shows how influential TV has become in our society.

Encouragement Indicator

DIY Stores	3%
Newspaper	4%
Friends	11%
Magazines	16%
Independent Stores	17%
Books	21%
TV	33%

The e-mailed newsletter has seen the most rapid growth over the last few years. It is sent out in large numbers for a relatively low cost. In the early days this was a unique way of communicating, but now many e-mailed newsletters are being deleted before they are read. The reason for this is the difficulty of keeping up with reading all the e-mails that are received these days. Keeping up with e-mails is now the biggest stress factor for business people. So, it may be difficult to get them to read your e-mail as well!

The traditional paper newsletter is still around and it is still effective. The design of the newsletter is critical to its success. People don't have much time to read, and the average person has a lot of 'reading' come through the post. Therefore you need to create a newsletter that is no more than a '7-minute read'.

The 7-minute read is the real key. Clients want an enjoyable seven minutes, any longer and it's straight in the wastepaper bin.

The following format works for our business and I recommend it for your business.

Key points for newsletter layout:

- No editorial — customers are not interested.
- Use lower case serif writing, like the newspaper.
- Keep words to 500-600 on the first page.
- Have one 'topical' exciting article.
- Fill the page with a relevant article.

- Keep to two or three stories in columns that are of interest to your readers. Keep them short and precise.

- Stories by customers or stories about what you can offer. Why not get team members to write stories?
- Don't be afraid to network articles with other organisations that your customers may use.

- Keep this to one-paragraph stories and items.

Warning: if you want to promote products in your newsletter, always promote them on a separate insert. Your acceptance rate will increase dramatically. We've tried both an insert and placing promotions inside the newsletter and have proved to ourselves that we can increase the uptake dramatically with an insert — it's worth the extra cost.

Say "Thank You" with a Thank You Card

In my opinion, "thank you" cards are under used. I discovered a company called "Thank You Cards Australia" a few years ago and I believe such cards are a brilliant marketing tool.

Look how "thank you" cards succeed from a consumer's perspective.

Let's visit Western Australia for this scenario. A customer visits "Bed Shed" (a bed retailer) in Perth and purchases a $1,000 bed. Two weeks later, Bed Shed will send its customer a "thank you" card. Inside the card, the customer has been given a choice of 15 restaurants to visit. All he or she has to do is to take a friend along to the restaurant, and they will receive a discount on the meal. With these "thank you" cards one business networks with another business to ensure everyone wins. The consumer is rewarded for dealing with Bed Shed by being given a discounted meal. Bed Shed builds customer loyalty, creating advocates and building a long-term relationship. The restaurant chosen gains two new customers, extra income from the visit, and the opportunity to build a relationship.

Thank You Cards Australia will set up promotional campaigns for retailers. If you are interested in this concept visit http://www.thankyoucards.com.au or e-mail Richard Joyce at richard.joyce@thankyoucards.com.au

Loyalty Cards

We've covered a number of permission marketing promotion campaigns without mentioning loyalty cards. The reason is that the majority of loyalty cards are actually discount cards.

Permission marketing promotions have an objective of increasing loyalty for businesses and increasing value for customers. Alas, most so-called loyalty cards fail at this.

Due to the amount of travelling I do, I found it beneficial to become a member of the Qantas Frequent Flyer club. The airlines were quick to join in with the loyalty club concept. As loyalty cards have evolved, the airlines have come up with some win:win campaigns without discounting the value of the product they sell, which is the air flight. In fact they can often make a profit out of my loyalty to them.

Let me explain. The flights I dread most are the Australia to London, or Australia to Los Angeles flights. As a small business owner, and a very frequent traveller, I can only justify paying Economy Class and I dread the thought of having my knees up around my chin for 15 hours (I'm quite tall).

On many flights, the airline on-sells my Economy Class seat to someone else and upgrades me to Business Class. This means it wins by selling one extra Economy Class seat that it would not have sold otherwise, and I win by enjoying the pleasures of a Business Class seat, including being able to stretch out my legs. The airline has not discounted its product, merely created another product it is able to sell (the Economy seat). It thus creates a win:win situation that leaves all parties smiling.

You need to create a similar scenario with your loyalty card members; do not give them a discount for spending money with you. If you discount to members, then you are offering a discount card, not a loyalty card.

People Are Your Key

People are the key to success. Your team members need to add notes to a customer's file every time they obtain information that is relevant to each customer. This means your database must be constantly being updated. It also means your sales team needs access to the database. This may unnerve some team members until they are fully trained in how to use the database, but it's the only way it will work.

At the same time the team members must be involved in the promotion. They may even manage it.

Some companies make sales team members responsible for a certain number of customers. These particular customers become 'their' customers, and the team member nurtures the relationships. The team members do the mail-outs and track the results. This is the ultimate in empowering your team. Companies that do this, such as "Nordstrom's" in the USA, would not have it any other way.

The manager's role is to assist the sales team. The sales team will need training, but its members also need the authorisation to make decisions and be subsequently accountable for this decision-making.

Memo

Are Your Customers Price-Drivers?

Research in the supermarket industry says 16% of your customers are. So why sell on price if the percentage is so small?

The same research says if you lose 2% of those customers to your competition, you could halve your net profit. Yes, that's why price is important.

Give each team member his or her own business card. Some companies prefer pre-printed cards with the team member's name printed on it. Other companies prefer business cards without a name printed on it so that each team member can write his or her name on it.

The system you select depends on your establishment's style, but do encourage the team to use the back of the business cards for notes. On my business card, I've actually put the word 'notes' and have lines printed underneath for people to write their notes on. Remember — business cards have two sides and you should make maximum use of both sides.

Think FOR Your Customer

Three Key Actions

- Introduce a trust policy into your business.
- Ensure you monitor the key TV programs that affect your business.
- Produce a seven-minute newsletter.

My Action Plan

1. _____

_____

_____

_____

_____

2. _____

_____

_____

_____

_____

3. _____

_____

_____

_____

_____

Yes, I Will Complain

Customers always complain! Shouldn't we encourage our clients to complain? A recent survey in the supermarket industry revealed 20% of customers in the store at any one time were dissatisfied with something. It may have been that they could not find a specific product, that there were queues at the checkout, the aisles were crowded or because 'that woman' is serving at the checkout. Most people always have something to complain about, however minor.

Memo

How Much Does It Cost You to Get a New Customer?

According to research carried out by Professor Frederick Reichheld and Phil Schefter, and detailed in their book 'The Loyalty Effect' it costs:

US$57 to get a new customer into an electronics shop

US$84 to get a new customer into a supermarket

US$53 to get a new customer into an apparel shop

How much is it costing you to get a new customer, client or patient?

Ref: Harvard Business Review, July/August 2000, pages 105-113.

Most people also feel that there is no point in complaining because nobody listens to them. Hence the chances are that you will not hear any complaints. If you're not getting complaints in your business, don't be complacent. It may be that the customer feels you're a non-listening business or that you haven't provided him with formal avenues for complaint.

Plus, most people feel they don't have the time to complain; 'it's simply not worth it', is a common feeling. In this situation, customers just move on and shop somewhere else. Loyalty is something that has to be earned in a society where consumers are becoming less loyal.

But, there is hope. Society is changing and this is an opportunity for everyone in business.

Complaints, Complaints, Complaints

Today people are complaining more often than ever, despite the effort involved. Gone are the days when consumers were prepared to put up with bad service. Now, more and more consumers are telling businesses what they think.

The British are known globally as a population that doesn't

complain about poor service. However, a survey reported in the *International Express* (Tuesday 8th May 2001, page 2) by Victoria Fletcher, shows that 50% of the British population complained about poor service in the year 2000.

What did they complain about? Their main complaints were about unhelpful staff and being forced to listen to answer-phone messages when contacting businesses.

One in five Brits claimed they would never go back to a business due to bad service; in fact 18% changed their bank or building society and 18% changed their supermarket.

Is this of concern? I think not — although it depends on how you look at it. Customers have always been dissatisfied, but now they are more likely to let you know about it. Look on this as a gift. The customer is now giving organisations the opportunity to address the situation; in the past customers didn't provide that opportunity.

This highlights what should be measured in business. It's not customer service that's the issue; it's customer satisfaction.

Barry Urquhart, an Australian marketing consultant, is reported in the *Business Review Weekly* magazine (June 15, 2001) as saying that the customer is not satisfied. His research in Australia shows:

- 56% of customers believe bank services declined in the last 12-month period.
- 49% of customers felt general retail services had declined in the last 12 months.
- 41% of customers believe telecommunications services had declined in the same period.

Plus 63% mentioned that their loyalty would improve if they believed that businesses were trying to correct the above decline.

How does your business fare in this situation? Carry out a customer survey and find out. But don't ask customers if they are satisfied or dissatisfied. This does not provide a true perspective. Customer use words such as: 'happy', 'angry', 'frustrated' and 'delighted'. They use emotional words; your survey should encourage them to describe their feelings and explain why they feel that way.

Memo

If You Can't Be Positive, Don't Say It

Customers want you to communicate with them in positive ways.

Signs such as 'Do Not Eat', 'Do Not Touch' and 'Trespassers Will Be Prosecuted' tend to result in customers registering the noun, ignoring the verb and therefore increasing the problem.

If you can't be positive or amusing when communicating what could be perceived as negative messages, you're better off not providing a sign in the first place.

Let me give you two of my favourite messages:

(1) 'Trespassers will be Prosecuted'

Was changed to:
'Trespassers will be propagated, pruned and potted.'

Ref: Zanthorrea Nursery, Western Australia.

(2) 'Don't leave your hotel, the natives are restless.'

Was changed to:
'Please note, as with any National celebration, there may be a small number of local participants who are a little too enthusiastic. As such, on Independence Day we would recommend taking advantage of the activities in the resort. Port Vila town centre would be best left for other days.'

Ref: Meridian Hotel memo on Wednesday, 30th July, Vanuatu Independence Day.

Your Complaints Policy

Complaints policies are a 'critical' part of customer service policy. The following key areas should be considered.

- Provide an opportunity for customers to share their thoughts with you. Not everyone will fill in a form and therefore you need to provide a variety of opportunities for your customer. These may include suggestion boxes, forms customers can mail in, or verbal comment opportunities.

- If customers complain or compliment you in writing and provide their name and address, then have a policy of replying within 24 hours. You don't have to agree but you do have to acknowledge the complaint.

- Empower your team to deal with complaints. Customers don't always want to talk to the boss.

- Train the team to deal with complaining customers. The key is to ensure they show empathy. Customers need to know that team members can relate to their problem.

- Remember that complaining customers need to feel they are being listened to. Make sure your team is a 'listening' team.

- Don't try to justify yourself, your company or your actions when a customer complains. Trying to justify an action shows the customer that you don't really want to hear what he has to say. Listen, empathise and solve. Never justify.

Think FOR Your Customer

Three Key Actions

- Complaints are a gift. Ensure your team members look on them that way.
- Encourage your customers to complain.
- Ensure complaints are addressed to the customers' satisfaction within 24 hours of receipt of the complaint.

My Action Plan

1. _____

_____

_____

_____

_____

2. _____

_____

_____

_____

_____

3. _____

_____

_____

_____

_____

The English Like to Queue

How often have you heard that whilst most nations hate queuing, the English like to line up?

As an Englishman, I'm of the opinion that none of us like to queue. I do accept that the tolerance level of some nations is higher, but road rage (loss of temper in car queues) is as big a problem in the UK as it is in other countries.

Every business needs a queue strategy. Hopefully, there are times in your business when you do get queues. The key is in managing those queues.

I came across an excellent queue management policy in Germany. It was three days after that dreadful day in 2001 when terrorists attacked New York. I was in Frankfurt airport trying to get a flight out to London. The queue time from check-in to security was about three hours, due to increased security checks following the attack. Perhaps you can appreciate what the atmosphere was like — pretty tense! I stood in line, prepared for my long wait. Within two minutes I was provided with a complimentary newspaper. I can't say the wait was any more enjoyable, but the opportunity to read whilst waiting removed a lot of the built-up tension.

Researchers tell us that stress levels increase when queues get longer than three people (three's a crowd); and the longer the queue, the greater the degree of stress people experience.

David Stewart-David researched 2,000 queues over a four-year period and in January 2003 produced his report 'The Stressful Queue'. His findings detailed consumers' emotional reactions to queues.

- Consumers are more likely to abandon a queue if they are queuing with a partner or a friend.
- Older people don't get so stressed in queues; they even use it as a social activity.
- The tolerance level of a queue for most adults is four minutes.

An Australian supermarket company introduced a major campaign a few years ago based on 'three's a crowd'. Its strategy was that it would open another checkout if a queue grew any longer than three people. Signs dangled around the store to emphasise the promise to the customer of opening another checkout if the queue

Memo

The McDonald's Formula

Why did this company dominate fast food?

They had a policy:

"This is the way we do things around here."

Do you have a similar policy?

It worked for McDonald's and took it around the globe.

was more than three people. The customers appreciated the promotion very much and were often heard to discuss this wonderful new campaign. Alas, the campaign did not last very long; in fact, it quickly disappeared. As in my local supermarket, the company could not keep its promise. At busy traffic times it was impossible to deliver the promise and customers began to complain to checkout operators, who were doing their best to cope with the situation. It was not the checkout operators who were at fault; it was management, making promises to customers that they could not deliver.

At the same time as this promotion was taking place in Australia, Feargal Quinn was introducing the same program into his supermarkets in Ireland. The difference was that he didn't tell the customers he was doing it — he just did it. As a result, the customers were impressed with the improvements. Feargal knew the key to queue management was just to improve the situation, without making promises to the customers that he may not have always been able to keep.

Feargal's policy was to ensure all his team members were on 'queue watch'. If the queue got too long, a member of the team had the power to get whatever he wanted to reduce the stress in the queue.

Queue stress-reducers could include:
- Cheese sampling trays
- Chocolate samples
- Other food samples
- Complimentary newspaper or coffee
- Promotional vouchers handed out
- Just going and having a chat

Plus, when you do reduce queues by opening a new checkout, you don't just say 'next' and watch the rush to join the next queue. The polite way for all concerned is to take the next person in line. Nothing annoys people more than seeing someone jump the queue and be served before them, when they have been waiting longer.

One system that can keep queues running smoothly is the 'snake' line, where people feed off at the front of the long queue to go to separate checkouts. The perception is that the queue is steadily moving and therefore you're progressing. If someone does cause a 'hold-up' at the checkout, the other checkouts will still process people. The reverse of this is a customer standing in the queue that gets held up. The customer becomes frustrated and annoyed whilst standing watching other lines moving more quickly through the other checkouts.

Think FOR Your Customer

Three Key Actions

- Ensure you have a positive queue (line) management policy.
- Ensure your checkout team members show empathy to customers who have to queue.
- Have a strong strategy in place for busy days.

My Action Plan

1. _____

_____

_____

_____

2. _____

_____

_____

_____

3. _____

_____

_____

_____

So You Can Answer the Phone

In my speaking engagements, I often mention the research that shows 70% of businesses lose trade because team members don't know how to correctly answer the phone. As you can imagine, I'm often confronted with puzzled looks while nearly everyone is thinking, "Who is this guy? Everyone knows how to answer a telephone!"

I accept that the majority of us are quite capable of answering a telephone socially. However, good telephone skills at work have to be learnt. Is your team building relations over the phone at work, where it really matters?

Answering the phone professionally in a business is a skill that many people fail to realise is a key factor in growing a business. We need to analyse this important skill in this section of the book.

The key to any task is to have the tools of the trade; without them your business will be perceived as unprofessional in the eyes of the customer. For this task, the tools of the trade are a phone, notepad and pen/pencil. How often have you rung somebody to hear "Just a minute, let me find a pen"? All the tools of the trade need to be gathered together. If pens have a tendency to 'walk', then hang them around the team members' necks. Having all the tools of trade on hand allows you to at least approach the task as a professional.

Once the tools are together, you wait for the phone to ring. In business, telephones should ring three times before they are answered. Answering the phone without allowing three rings often means the person on the other end of the line is not ready for your response. But for every ring after three rings, the person trying to contact you is left waiting, resulting in more negative thoughts concerning your business. Consider what this person is thinking about your business after 15 rings — if he waits that long!

Are Answer-Phone and Automated Voices the Solution?

People like talking to people; they generally do not like talking to machines. If you're a people-orientated business, then throw those automated voice machines away. They are not helping your customers; they are more likely frustrating them.

The machines may be saving your business money in the short term, but they are definitely not building long-term relations for your business. What you need is a system that builds a relationship, not destroys it. Research in Australia by Barry Urquhart in 2002 identified that 38% of Australians hate queuing on the phone and listening to recorded messages. Compare this to the 17% of Australians who use the word 'hate' when describing how they feel about physically queuing in shops. Customers want to talk to positive, friendly people. When customers walk into your business, they make a decision about your business using their eyes and their ears. On the telephone, that positive, friendly team member's only opportunity to get the right message across is to smile prior to opening his or her mouth. SMILING BEFORE AND DURING ANSWERING THE PHONE IS OBLIGATORY when you are in the business of building relationships.

The next stage is deciding *what* to say, as we now know *how* to say it. I'm not a believer in phone scripts, as scripted lines always come across insincerely. But I am a believer in getting the 'opener' across as a company policy. In our own business the policy is to answer the phone with a welcome, the company name, then the first name of person talking.

Eg *"Good morning, John Stanley Associates, this is Jenni"*.

The opener, apart from being a greeting, allows the other person to get used to accents or dialects and the fact that a 'real' person has answered the phone.

The company name gives the caller an indication that he has reached his intended target, whilst the offering of a first name gives the caller a point of contact and encourages him to provide his own name.

Now we can get into the meat of the conversation. If you're like me, you'll forget names and key points whilst people are talking. This is where the paper and pen are valuable. Jot down the caller's name and key points of the conversation so that you can refer back to them during and after the conversation. Apart from that, the conversation should be natural. Don't have scripts, let people be themselves; this will build relationships more quickly than anything else.

However, the close of the conversation is a real key area, and full of pitfalls for the unprofessional phone user. Firstly, summarise the main points and reach an agreement with the caller on the course of action; and then do what you say you will do.

We've all experienced the situation in which a supplier has said he will phone us back within a specified time frame. But how often do people do what they say they will do? Not very often! The key to success is quite simple. If you say you'll phone back at a specific time, then do so.

This may mean keeping a phone records book. Having one means that other members of the team should have access to the book and be empowered to make the appropriate decisions in your unforeseen absence.

'Think FOR Your Customer' policy, implemented as a phone strategy, can save your customers a great deal of stress. Plus, you can become one of those rare businesses that are a pleasure to do business with over the phone.

Memo

Kaizen

'Kaizen' is the real key to managing change. Kaizen is a Japanese word that is difficult to translate exactly into English. It basically means that the key to success is to make small, seemingly insignificant, on-going and never-ending improvements in order to continue to grow your business or your life.

Think FOR Your Customer

Three Key Actions

- Train all your team members in the skills of answering the phone professionally.
- Make sure you've provided all the tools necessary so everyone can answer the phone in a professional manner.
- Don't introduce answering services unless it is absolutely unavoidable.

My Action Plan

1. _____

   _____

   _____

   _____

2. _____

   _____

   _____

   _____

3. _____

   _____

   _____

   _____

SECTION 8

Praise the Team, Not the Customer

The challenge in providing exceptional customer service is to be an effective leader. A leader's objective is to maximise the output of the team and to grow the team so that individuals give of their best.

One of the best books on leadership is *'The Leadership Challenge'* by Knowze and Posner (Gossey Bass Publishers, San Francisco, ISBN 0787901105). This book looks at the role of leadership in all aspects of management. I want to concentrate on looking at the leadership of your team.

As a leader, you should recognise the individual's contribution to the success of your business.

Rewards should be based on a measured success strategy. Most retail businesses take their total retail sales, divide this by the number of customers and arrive at an average sale per customer. When team members exceed this average sale they are rewarded. But is this the way forward?

Why not let your team members set their own measurements? By all means you should tell them the average sale per customer, but then let them set their own targets. You'll often find they will provide a higher baseline than you would have set them. If I, as a sales team member, set a standard, the chances are I'll exceed what I've set. Rewards should 'kick in' when the individual exceeds the target he or she has set.

When rewarding individuals, be as creative as possible about the reward. It is critical that you personally get involved with the celebrations when the target is reached or exceeded.

Always praise and recognise achievements in public and reprimand team members in private. Public praise is doubly worth having — public criticism is de-motivating.

Many companies have an 'Employee of the Month' award that they recognise and celebrate with their customers. This creates heroes for your customers and your team.

Have a policy of catching people doing something right, rather than walking the shop floor trying to catch people doing something wrong.

Saint Francis Hospital in Memphis, Tennessee, USA has a 'Caught Caring' policy. When team members are caught caring they are presented with 'Caught Caring' pins. This is a simple but effective means of identifying and rewarding positive behaviour in individuals.

The Caught in the Act Award

The role of a leader is to provide guidance and reward success. If you are going to empower your team to delight customers then your team members should be rewarded for their successes.

"Stauffers" garden centre in Kassel Hills, Pennsylvania, USA has introduced CITA (Caught in the Act) awards. Management awards these to team members who are observed on the shop floor delighting customers. The award is presented to the team member directly after the outstanding event and the team member puts the CITA award into a monthly draw for a $50 voucher.

What I like about this is that it forces management to get onto the shop floor and examine what is really happening. Plus, the objective is to catch team members exceeding expectations and instantly recognising the achievement.

This is a far more inspiring style of management than those who are trying to 'catch the team members out' doing something wrong.

Is your management trying to reward team members for exceeding company standards?

Give People Responsibility

"Ritz-Carlton Hotels" in the USA, a winner of the Malcolm Baldrige National Quality Awards, ensures its associates have the power to make decisions. Team members at the registration desk, a key position in the business, have the authority to correct any error up to the value of $2,000 without approval from managers.

Compare this with a situation I came across recently in a hardware store I was consulting at in New Zealand. During the morning a young sales assistant made a $350 sale. That same person interrupted my work with the manager during the afternoon to tell him that he had a problem to resolve. It turned out that a customer had returned to the store with a faulty product. The product value was less than $20. Only the manager had the authority to deal with it. It was beyond my comprehension that a company could trust a team member with a $350 decision in the morning, but not with a $20 decision in the afternoon!

Empowerment is the Name of the Game

People must be empowered to make decisions. In the majority of cases, they will make decisions in favour of both the company and the customer.

Prior to empowering people, give them the guidelines and tools they need. Given the rules of the game, team members will play by the rules. Everyone should be able to make decisions with the customer, to a specific monetary value.

If you don't make the rules clear to everyone, it's amazing what can happen.

My favourite incident, which I often relate in conferences, happened to a colleague of mine in the United Kingdom. She was shopping in a local pharmacy (drug store) and purchased a pack of ten plasters (band-aids). At home, she found the pack only contained nine plasters. The next day she happened to be passing the pharmacy and thought she would let the pharmacist know, in case it happened again. She went in and saw an assistant, who quickly responded "let me get a manager". My colleague stood around in the store for five minutes (which seems an eternity when you actually do it) before a 'manager' appeared and welcomed the customer with the comment "I gather you have a problem". My colleague explained the situation, whereupon the manager went to the shelf, picked up a new box of plasters, counted ten out, ripped one off, gave it to her and put the box back on the shelf! I believe that, statistically, if he kept repeating this practice, every box in the pharmacy would quickly be in the same condition!

Many leaders look on their role as being a coach or cheerleader for the team. You know that you've developed the team, when as the leader you are not the customers' favourite salesperson and your average sale is lower than other team members average sale.

That's the real challenge — ensuring the team's members are better than you at increasing the average sale. Some managers may find that concept a little unnerving, but they are managers — they are not leaders. Leaders aim to grow the team to ensure that the team members are the ones that shine. Your role is to make yourself redundant in the selling process.

Think FOR Your Customer

Three Key Action Points

- Always try to catch team members doing something right and reward them in public.
- Always reprimand team members in private.
- Provide the rules of the game to your team, so they know what they can and can't do, as well as the standards they have to exceed.

My Action Plan

1. _____

_____

_____

2. _____

_____

_____

3. _____

_____

_____

_____

SECTION 9

Take Yourself Forward Five Years

Welcome to Your New World!

Happy New Year! Hasn't the world changed since you first started reading this book?

In the intervening years we've lost some famous business names, some of which we were all convinced would make it to this celebration. Where did they go wrong, and why did you survive?

Once upon a time we were convinced that technology and the digital revolution were the answer. We now know that they were tools, which if used correctly would help us survive — but they were not the complete answer.

Survivors realised that people are social animals. Historically, a lot of social contact was via events like church fairs, and then shopping malls. Many of our previous social contact points have gone and now people are looking to individual businesses like yours to provide that all-important human contact.

But you also know it's more than human contact that ensured your business's survival. New-age consumers are more stressed than they have ever been in the past.

The political turmoil that started in 2001 has made consumers less confident and more uncertain of a world that can seemingly change in minutes. Research gurus of the last decade informed us that consumers would have more leisure time than ever, when in fact that leisure time has decreased and has become something to savour because it is now so precious.

In addition, look at all the information that consumers are expected to absorb. The information available in one colour supplement of a weekend newspaper is equivalent to a whole year's information for a consumer living two centuries ago. There is no way that consumers today are up-to-date with what your business is doing.

So today you are dealing with consumers who are more stressed, more time-poor and armed with less overall information that they have ever been — even though there is more information available to them than at any other point in history.

You were aware of these changes, which is why you implemented a policy to 'Think FOR Your Customer', as this was a survival strategy for your business.

The implementation of this strategy obviously meant major changes within your business and it is worth summarising those changes at this point.

Your De-Stress Policy

Stress comes from factors lying both outside of and within your control. You show empathy to customers over stress factors outside your control, especially as these cause you as much stress as they do your customers.

Memo

Your Business Could Be A World Champion

Businesses are the same as sports champions; to be the world's best you need four traits:

(1) The Desire and Vision to be the best

(2) High Expectations; you're always chasing, because you never get there

(3) Perseverance

(4) Honesty, with oneself and others

You have the opportunity to change the outcomes.

Ref: Roy Brett Rutledge, New Zealand
brett@rutledge.co.nz

But, more critically, you've eliminated most of the internal factors that cause consumers stress. You now manage your queues more effectively; you have created a positive business ambience by careful use of well-chosen music, aroma, lighting and space.

You've made your team clearly visible to your consumers and created a layout that is easy for your customers to visit, browse and find what they are looking for.

You have regular customer forums to address the changing nature of your customers' stresses, as you realise that a stressed customer will spend less money with your business and more with your competition.

Your Time Investment Policy

Time is a precious resource for your customers, so you've taken on the digital revolution and adapted it wherever it will save your customers time. Home delivery and 'Do It for Me' strategies in your business are major features that distinguish you from your competition. Your strategy is to appreciate that time is of the essence to your customers and that your objective is to save time when they are dealing with you, so that they can enjoy more of their limited leisure time.

Your Information Strategy

You appreciate that customers don't have the information they need to make sound decisions. Yes, it's freely available to them, but your strategy has been to build a relationship of trust with your customers. Your customers trust you to think for them and to make their decision process quicker and easier. They still want to be part of the thinking process, but rely on your assistance to quickly make the appropriate decision to suit their needs.

These customers appreciate that your business has the answers to all their questions, but often they don't even know what questions to ask. Today's customer really relies on the relationship of trust that has been built between you both, knowing that your business will meet all his needs.

This trust has been built on both the use of technology and on team commitment.

You are a 'high-tech, high-touch' business that truly '*Thinks FOR the Customer*'.

Think FOR Your Customer

Three Key Actions

- Plan the next three years in your business and career.
- Stress on customers will increase; ensure your policies are aimed at de-stressing them.
- Implement ideas from this book — go and... DO IT!

My Action Plan

1. _____

   _____

   _____

   _____

   _____

2. _____

   _____

   _____

   _____

   _____

3. _____

   _____

   _____

   _____

   _____

Best selling book by the authors

JUST ABOUT EVERYTHING A RETAIL MANAGER NEEDS TO KNOW

Every so often something really useful comes along. And, for retail managers, *Just About Everything a Retail Manager Needs to Know* is it. By distilling just about everything relating to successful management practice into practical and immediately accessible how-to's, this book provides answers to your retail challenges and questions in straightforward language with the minimum of fuss. If you, as a retailer, needed to own just one reference tool, then *Just About Everything a Retail Manager Needs to Know* is it!

This book is an essential tool for the new or experienced retailer.

Just About Everything a Retail Manager Needs to Know provides ideas, even for the most experienced retailer. None of us can learn all the skills of retailing at one time and be proficient at them all. This book helps you develop your existing strengths and improve your weaknesses. It provides ideas and advice for when you have a problem that needs solving.

This book should be shared by your team.

Just About Everything a Retail Manager Needs to Know is a book that won't sit on your shelf gathering dust. It is a tool your whole team will refer to constantly.

Leave a copy in the staff room and let your team find a solution in it to problems as they occur. It can help you improve the retailing skills of your whole team.

Just About Everything a Retail Manager Needs to Know,
John Stanley, 2003

Other recent books by the authors

THE COMPLETE GUIDE TO GARDEN CENTER MANAGEMENT
Ball Publishing, Chicago, USA, 2002

As a contributing author – John Stanley
CONFESSIONS OF SHAMELESS INTERNET PROMOTERS
Success Showcase Publishing, Tempe, USA, 2002
THE MODERN PUBLIC LIBRARY BUILDING – MANAGING, PLANNING
Libraries Unlimited Press, Westport, USA, 2002

Video by John Stanley and Pete Luckett
WINNING AT RETAIL
Pete Luckett Inc/John Stanley Associates, 2003

For information on any of these books or videos, contact info@johnstanley.cc or phone John Stanley Associates' office in Australia on +61 (8) 9293 4533 or fax +61 (8) 9293 4561.

Frequently Asked Questions

Here are some of the most frequently asked questions after people have been exposed to the Stanley's concepts…

Q: **How can I book John as a speaker at my next conference or seminar?**

A: John is a dynamic, charismatic and highly sought after speaker, who tailors his presentations to suit his audience needs and culture. John specializes in the retail and service industries. Send an email to John Stanley Associates office to info@johnstanley.cc, fax +61 (8) 9293 4561, or call +61 (8) 9293 4533 to talk to a team member direct.

Q: **Will John come and give me advice on my business, or train my team?**

A: John has been consulting to management and training teams for over 25 years. He has clients in 17 countries and travels the world several times each year. If you would like to enlist John to help your organisation then please email info@johnstanley.cc to discuss your needs or fax +61 (8) 9293 4561.

Q: **How can I obtain more copies of this book?**

A: This book can be ordered online at www.johnstanley.cc. Send an email to info@johnstanley.cc if you would like to discuss discounts for bulk orders.

Q: **Can this book be translated into other languages?**

A: Previous books that John has written have been translated under licence into other languages. Please email John Stanley Associates to discuss this possibility.

Q: **What subjects does John talk on at conferences?**

A: John specializes in the retail and services industries, and will talk on anything relevant to those sectors. In particular he has spoken on Creating Lifetime Customers, Effective Selling Techniques, Managing your Business and Promoting Your Products or Services.

Visit John Stanley Associates website and register for a free online newsletter to receive the latest tips and ideas for the retail and services industries. www.johnstanley.cc

Are your team creating loyal customers, or just serving people?

Do your customers go away and rave to their friends about your amazing service?

Is your business turnover exploding through word of mouth?

Are your sales team excited and enthusiastic about coming to work each day?

Do your clientele love to visit your store and interact with your team?

If you are not sure that you can answer "Yes!" to any of these questions, read on.

John Stanley has been motivating teams to push enterprises to greater heights through enthusiasm, self-empowerment and increased awareness of customer needs.

Whatever your objectives, John Stanley can help fast track your business to reach amazing new heights. His valuable, practical and instantly effective ideas are based on over 25 years of international retail experience and ongoing international research.

With John's mentoring, training and on-site consultancy, small retail stores have grown into professional multi-million dollar business operations, while large international companies use John's skills to improve their professionalism and develop consistency throughout their stores.

John Stanley is one of few consultants in the world today who have the credibility, international knowledge and such a clear understanding of what today's customers are demanding and what retailers need to know to become more profitable.

John can help you achieve all this, and more....

Testimonials

"John Stanley re-designed our Farm shop to improve customer flow, merchandising and general image. As a result of the re-design we have achieved a 44% increase in turnover, and 18% increase in customer numbers, and a 22% increase in average spend over the same period last year. All this in spite of the current difficult trading time due to the Foot and Mouth outbreak here in the UK. We are also finding that running the shop is much easier and less stressful on many levels – especially stock control. Long may it continue. Thanks again for all your help – you inspire!!"
Stuart Beare, Tulleys Farm, United Kingdom

"I employed John Stanley as a consultant to work with my team on developing the overall appearance of the store. As a result of John's input and advice, within six months we achieved a growth that far exceeded our expectations. On a busy day we are achieving a turnover which is equivalent to one weeks turnover prior to us taking over the store."
Pierre Sequeira, 'Store of the Year 2001', Supa Valu Como, Western Australia

For more information on John Stanley Associates services contact:

John Stanley Associates, 142 Hummerston Road, Kalamunda, WA 6076 Australia

Tel: +61 8 9293 4533 Fax: +61 8 9293 4561
Email: info@johnstanley.cc
or visit the website at www.johnstanley.cc